MARK F. FISCHER
MARY MARGARET RALEY
editors

FOUR WAYS
TO BUILD MORE
Effective
PARISH
COUNCILS

A Pastoral Approach

TWENTY-THIRD PUBLICATIONS
185 WILLOW STREET • PO BOX 180 • MYSTIC, CT 06355
TEL: 1-800-321-0411 • FAX: 1-800-572-0788
Bayard   E-MAIL: ttpubs@aol.com • www.twentythirdpublications.com

Twenty-Third Publications
A Division of Bayard
185 Willow Street
P.O. Box 180
Mystic, CT 06355
(860) 536-2611
(800) 321-0411
www.twentythirdpublications.com

Copyright ©2002 Conference for Pastoral Planning and Council Development. All rights reserved. No part of this publication may be reproduced in any manner without prior written permission of the publisher. Write to the Permissions Editor.

ISBN:1-58595-194-3
Library of Congress Catalog Card Number: 2001135544
Printed in the U.S.A.

Acknowledgments

The collaborative effort to produce this book extends well beyond the authors and editors to include the support of the membership of the Conference for Pastoral Planning and Council Development at all stages of development. Past executive directors, Art Deegan and Fran Schumer, ASC, gave their encouragement and guidance in the early days of the project. Siobhan Verbeek, Associate Director of the Secretariat for Doctrine and Pastoral Practices reviewed the manuscript, making several helpful suggestions. Mary Montgomery, representing the Coordinating Committee of CPPCD, and Mary Gindhart of the Archdiocese of Philadelphia also made suggestions for improving the finished manuscript. They deserve a special word of thanks. Thanks also to Tom Artz of ACTA Publications for his help in preparing the final manuscript.

Contents

Introduction 1

Part I: Understanding the Job 9

Chapter One: Working Together to Build an Effective Parish 11
Mark F. Fischer

Chapter Two: A Spirituality for Councils 23
Loughlan Sofield

Part II: Involving the Right People 41

Chapter Three: Involving the Right People:
Selecting Parish Pastoral Council Members 43
Marian Schwab

Chapter Four: Pastoral Planning: Involving the Whole Community 61
George Wilson

Part III: Doing the Research 85

Chapter Five: Appreciative Inquiry:
A Powerful Process for Parish Listening and Planning 87
David DeLambo and Richard Krivanka

Chapter Six: Demographic Information as an Aid to Parish Planning 102
George Cobb

Part IV: Planning for the Future 117

Chapter Seven: Planning: Idol or Icon of Pastoral Councils? 119
John Flaherty

Chapter Eight: How Do We Get There From Here? A Planning Model 137
Mary Margaret Raley

Chapter Nine: Sharing More Than a Pastor 161
Mary Montgomery

Chapter Ten: The Culturally Integrated Council 182
Mark F. Fischer and María Elena Uribe

Notes 194
About the Authors 200
Bibliography 205
Index 211

Four Ways to Build
More Effective Parish Councils

Introduction

Elena Rodriguez, the secretary at St. Mary's Church, testifies that the parish is a busy place. She knows what she is talking about. She maintains the parish calendar, and whenever the calendar changes, Elena feels the repercussions. Exceptionally active parishioners complain when scheduling conflicts prevent them from attending events they are interested in. Catechists compete for limited meeting space. The pastor, Father MacAller, encourages parishioners to participate in the Sunday liturgies as greeters, ushers, readers, eucharistic ministers, and choir members. Each of these ministries demands periodic meetings. Elena not only has to juggle the parish calendar, but coordinate it with the personal calendar of Father MacAller. He likes to drop in on meetings, never staying for very long, visiting from one group to another, greeting people and listening to the conversations.

On the first Monday of every month, however, Father MacAller does not visit around. He spends the entire evening with his pastoral council. He commits himself to the council because it enables him to meet with representative parishioners to engage in pastoral planing. Father MacAller calls this his "principal form of collaboration, dialogue, and discernment," echoing the words of Pope John Paul II's *Christifideles laici,* which describes pastoral councils at the diocesan level.

Pastoral councils are an important part of American Catholic life, existing in more than 15,000 U.S. parishes. Why are they so important? This collection of essays offers an explanation. And it presents four principles that make councils even more effective. Effective councils understand their job, involve the right people, research pastoral matters, and plan for the future.

Understanding the Job

Whenever Father MacAller meets with his pastoral council, he repeats to the members their purpose. "Vatican II gave pastoral councils three general tasks," he says. "They investigate pastoral matters, ponder them, and formulate practical conclusions concerning them." Then, with a look at each councillor, he adds: "If you're not investigating, pondering, and formulating, you're not doing your job."

Understanding the job of the pastoral councillor is the opening theme of this collection of essays. The first essay is "Working Together to Build an Effective Parish." Some people argue that pastoral councils ought to limit themselves to spiritual matters or long-range visioning. The first essay takes another tack. Written by Mark F. Fischer of St. John's Seminary in the Archdiocese of Los Angeles, it argues that nothing should infringe upon the freedom of pastors to consult as they see fit about pastoral matters in the parish. The second essay is entitled "The Spirituality of Councils." In it, Trinitarian Brother Loughlan Sofield states that council spirituality is not about withdrawing from the world into a realm of abstract piety. No, it is a shared discernment about the reality of the parish. Good councillors imbue their work of pastoral planning with the spirituality of Jesus and the apostles. These first two essays clarify the job of the pastoral council. As Father MacAller told the pastoral council at St. Mary's, it is the job of investigating, pondering, and formulating practical conclusions.

This threefold job looks simple and straightforward. But Father MacAller's secretary, Elena Rodriguez, will tell you that it is not. When the council begins to study a pastoral matter, tensions sometimes arise. Elena knows from personal experience that loyalty, friendship, and hard work are needed to hold the group together. Part of her job is to prepare documents for the pastoral council. This starts with the council's agenda. One would think that an agenda is the simplest thing of all. Not Elena. She knows that, in order to create an agenda, Father MacAller and the council chairperson, vice-chairperson, and secretary have to meet within two weeks of the council meeting. They must decide what the council should do when it gets together next. If the pastor and officers take longer than two weeks, Elena cannot mail the agenda (plus the minutes from the last meeting and other documents) in a timely fashion.

Involving the Right People

The formation of the council agenda hinges upon more people, however, than just the pastor and the council officers. It depends on the readiness of the other councillors as well. In an important way, the agenda depends on the entire parish. Father MacAller and Elena Rodriguez learned that from experience. A prudent agenda reflects the importance of council matters and the capacity of councillors to undertake them. If the matters are unimportant—that is, if the parishioners of St. Mary's do not see their relevance to the parish's well being—they are unworthy of the council's time. And if the council is not ready to study and reflect on them, they do not belong on the council agenda. Forming the council agenda is a matter of judgment. A good judgment reflects the involvement of good people.

Involving the right people is the second theme of this book. Who are the right people for the pastoral council? Marian Schwab, Director of Pastoral Planning for the Diocese of Houma-Thibodeaux, Louisiana, answers that question in Chapter Three, entitled "Involving the Right People: Selecting Parish Pastoral Council Members." The right people, she says, are those who can do the job. They understand why the pastor wants to consult a council and what the pastor is consulting about. The pastor, in turn, understands how to engage the whole community in identifying and selecting new councillors. "Pastoral Planning: Involving the Whole Community" is the title of Chapter Four by Jesuit Father George Wilson, a consultant with the Management Design Institute. His chapter emphasizes that pastoral planning empowers the community and builds trust. Pastoral councils facilitate pastoral planning, he says, but should never undertake it in isolation from other parishioners. Rather, good councils know when to consult other people in order to build a common vision. Planning fails if it does not involve the right people, both councillors and parishioners in general.

Doing the Research

Pastoral planning is shorthand for the task of investigating, reflecting, and recommending practical conclusions. Wise pastors like Father MacAller know that this threefold task means different things to different people. He learned this the hard way. When he was a new pastor, he asked his council to "investigate" the parish's religious education program, which was outgrowing the parish's facilities. Father MacAller had envisioned that councillors would interview the Director of Religious Education and a few of the parish catechists. He had also requested that they visit religious education programs in neighboring parishes, where home-based catechesis was flourishing. His hope was that the investigation might develop plans to expand religious education without the construction of a new parish building. Father MacAller assumed that the council's "investigation" would be a limited and positive experience.

The investigation turned out to be anything but limited and positive. At that time, an unhappy parishioner with a grudge chaired the council. Unknown to Father MacAller, the chairman was dissatisfied with his daughter's religious education. He conducted the investigation like an inquisition. He planned interviews with every catechist. The first interviews were more like interrogations designed to expose the catechists' weaknesses. The catechists were soon up in arms and Father MacAller had to stop the process. The chairman resigned. The DRE, Elena's long-time friend, almost resigned as well, and only stayed because Elena pleaded with her to be patient. It was a difficult time to say the least. The investigation alienated many parishioners. And to add insult to injury, Father MacAller learned that he could not escape the need to construct a new facility. If he had only spoken with a city planner, he would have discovered that new home construction in the city was about to swell the population. It would make the old religious education facility hopelessly inadequate, even if some parishioners were to provide home-based catechesis. Research and investigation by the council, Father MacAller found, is both important and delicate.

Doing the research is the third theme in this collection of essays. Parish research should be anything but an impersonal and potentially alienating process of investigation, according to David DeLambo and Richard Krivanka. These pastoral planners from the Diocese of Cleveland call their chapter "Appreciative Inquiry: A Powerful Process for Parish Listening and Planning." In it, they propose that pastoral planning should not start with a focus on parish problems. Rather, it should begin with appreciation for the faith that has formed the community in the first place. In such an appreciative climate research and planning can build up the parish. George Cobb, Director of Planning for the Diocese of Charlotte, provides a good illustration of this. His chapter, entitled "Demographic Information as an Aid to Parish Planning," asks what Census 2000 data can do for the parish. The answer is that it can do a great deal and at very little cost. Demographic information helps pastors and councils know the parish. That is the first step in effective pastoral planning. Research is essential to planning, not a luxury for councils with time on their hands.

Planning for the Future

Back at St. Mary's Church, the council never has time on its hands. That is because Father MacAller constantly raises new questions. He jots them down in a spiral notebook that he keeps in his pocket. Then, when he meets with Elena Rodriguez, he asks her to pass them on to the pastoral council chairwoman. "I thought my frequent calls to the chairwoman were a pain in the neck, but she gave me a different perspective," said Elena. "She told me that whenever Father MacAller asks a question, he shows his reliance on the council." The chairwoman's remark to Elena underscored the nature of parish pastoral planning. At its heart is a desire to anticipate the future and respond in a Christlike way.

Planning for the future is the fourth theme of this book. Some people have the mistaken idea that planning is an abstract exercise designed to keep councils busy. It can even seem like an end in itself. John Flaherty, Director of Research and Planning for the Diocese of Pittsburgh, disputes that. In his chapter, entitled "Planning: Idol or Icon of Pastoral Councils?" he likens planning to a religious icon. Pastoral planning is a ministry designed to focus parish attention on the gospel. It transports the parish from mere self-maintenance to gospel-based commitments. The transportation metaphor arises in "How Do We Get There From Here? A Planning Model," the title of the chapter written by Mary Margaret Raley. Raley, former Director of Parish Planning for the Diocese of Fort Worth, likens planning to a family vacation. Just as a family must plan if it wants to get to Yellowstone National Park, so the parish must plan if it wants to proclaim its faith to its members and to the wider community.

No contemporary treatment of pastoral councils is complete without attention to the decline in the number of priests and to the multicultural reality of U.S. Catholicism. *Diocesan Efforts at Parish Reorganization,* a 1995 study by the Conference for Pastoral Planning and Council Development, found 19 dioceses in which ten percent or more of parishes were without a resident pastor. What impact does this have on pastoral councils? Dominican Sister Mary Montgomery, Director of Pastoral Planning for the Archdiocese of Dubuque, knows how her diocese responded. In a chapter entitled "Sharing More than a Pastor," she describes how small groups of Dubuque parishes have developed "cluster councils" to advise the pastor responsible for the cluster. Such councils are one response to the priest shortage.

The role of immigrant parishioners is important for councils as well. According to the 2000 study *Catholicism USA,* from 1991-96 a majority of immigrants to the U.S. came from Latin America and a significant minority came from Asia. Many of these immigrants are Catholics, and some become pastoral council members. The consequences are explored in "The Culturally Integrated Council," the chapter written by Mark F. Fischer and María Elena Uribe, Coordinator of the pastoral councils office for the Archdiocese of Los Angeles. They argue that parishes should not establish separate councils for each immigrant group, but strive to create a single pastoral council that reflects all parishioners and fosters pastoral planning for the entire parish.

About this Book

In 1995 *Developing a Vibrant Parish Pastoral Council* appeared in bookstores. It was a collection of essays edited by Arthur X. Deegan, II, Executive Director of the Conference of Pastoral Planning and Council Development (CPPCD). Each of the eleven contributors was a member of the CPPCD, the national organization that promotes pastoral planning and ongoing development of pastoral councils. The book was a success and went through two printings.

Five years later, CPPCD members agreed that it was time for a new collection. Sister M. Frances Schumer, ASC, Art Deegan's successor, authorized the initial steps. She was succeeded in turn by Maria Rodgers

O'Rourke, who encouraged the completion of the project. Contributors were selected from among those who had made presentations at the annual CPPCD conventions. Each of the contributors has assisted the development of parish and diocesan pastoral councils for many years. Many of them work in diocesan offices. They come from all parts of the country, including the East (Pittsburgh), the South (Louisiana), predominately rural dioceses (Charlotte and Dubuque), and those with rapidly growing populations (Texas and California). The chapters reflect their experience in helping councils deal with the issues that face them.

Each author was invited to reflect on his or her experience with councils. Some of the topics include basic teaching about councils, such as their purpose and spirituality. Other topics include difficult and pressing issues facing councils today, such as the sharing of a single priest by multiple parishes and multicultural councillors. Each author shares ideas, exercises, tools, or insights that have been useful.

Father MacAller and Elena Rodriguez are fictional characters in the imaginary parish of St. Mary's. But their experience with the parish pastoral council is typical. Councils are numerous and influential because U.S. Catholics believe in the job they do. Bishops recognize their value, and most bishops mandate them. Parish participants in the work of councils make an important contribution to the church. Vatican II said that pastoral councils begin by investigating pastoral matters under the bishop's direction, reflecting on them, and formulating practical conclusions. This book affirms what Vatican II said. When councils understand their task, involve the right people, do their research, and plan for the future, they help pastors like Father MacAller, staff members like Elena Rodriguez, and parishes everywhere carry on the mission of the church.

PART 1

Understanding the Job

CHAPTER ONE

Working Together to Build an Effective Parish

Mark F. Fischer

Participants in pastoral councils are part of a large and powerful movement in the U.S. church. This movement began more than thirty-five years ago with the documents of Vatican II that recommended the establishment of councils. There have been efforts in the past to estimate the number of parish councils. As early as 1970, Charles A. Fecher, writing on behalf of the National Council of Catholic Men, estimated that there were already 10,000 councils in the U.S., or roughly a council in every other parish. By 1976, some were even suggesting that three-fourths of American parishes had such councils. Ten years later, a reliable sociological survey confirmed this figure. The *Notre Dame Study of Catholic Parish Life*, based on a survey of 1,099 parishes, stated that three-fourths of all parishes have a parish council "or its equivalent." And recently the *National Parish Inventory Project Report* stated that "More than nine in ten parishes report having a parish pastoral council."[1] If this is true, then the number of parish councils is very large indeed. American Catholics have affirmed the recommendations of the Vatican II bishops.

Two Misunderstandings

Despite the large number of councils, there is little popular agreement about their scope and purpose. Indeed, there are many misunderstandings about them. For example, some may be tempted to think that the business of pastoral councils is merely with immediate administrative matters. According to this misconception, the practical matters of the council are the mundane matters of parish maintenance, scheduling, committee life, or social affairs. The assumption behind this view is that administrative matters are the only matters of which lay Catholics are capable. More than that, some might think, Catholic parishioners cannot handle.

This first misconception needs to be cleared up. Yes, the matter of the pastoral council is practical. But it is practical in this way: it has to do with practical matters and leads to action. Pastoral matters do not dwell in the land of theory. To be sure, it is beyond the competence of pastoral councils "to decide on general questions bearing on faith, orthodoxy, moral principles or laws of the universal Church."[2] But most councils avoid these questions. They focus on pastoral matters. Pastoral matters have to do with the life and choices of the parish. We make a mistake when we say that pastoral matters, the matters treated by the council, are mundane, unspiritual, and inconsequential because they are practical. In fact, I will argue that almost nothing of practical relevance is beyond the scope of a well-formed and well-chosen pastoral council. That is my first argument.

My second has to do with another popular misunderstanding. It is the mistake that councils should limit themselves to dreaming and visioning. According to this view, the business of the council is the construction of mission statements, goals, and plans for the distant future—but irrelevant to the parish's present reality. Dreaming and visioning is the work of the council, in this mistaken opinion, because the scope of councils must be limited. People of this opinion always remind councils that they are not the final decision makers in the parish, as if their work has nothing to do with decision making. They constantly repeat that councils are consultative only, as if that meant that the work of the council has no practical relevance. They confine councils to dreaming and visioning in order to limit the councillors' expectations. "Don't get your hopes up about making a substantial difference," they seem to say. "The council is consultative only."

Against the misunderstanding that councils are only dreamers and visionaries, I want to make another argument about the right use of councils. Unless councils are involved in practical decisions with important consequences, they are wasting their time. Wise pastors consult because they want to make sound decisions about the life of the parish. Pastors consult because they know that they do not know everything. Pastors consult because they want the wisdom of their people.

Vatican II and the Code of Canon Law do not give exhaustive advice to pastoral councils.[3] Parish pastoral councils, says canon 536, help the pastor to promote pastoral activity. They do so under the norms established by the diocesan bishop. There is not much more in canon 536 about the purpose of councils than that. But the canons about *diocesan* pastoral councils give an insight into what the bishops at Vatican II envisioned for pastoral councils in general. Canon 511 states that diocesan pastoral councils are to investigate, reflect, and propose practical conclusions. This threefold description is taken from the Vatican II *Decree on the Pastoral Office of Bishops*, no. 27. It has been consistently applied to diocesan pastoral councils and was first extended to *parish* pastoral councils by the Congregation for the Clergy in 1973. It is more specific than canon 536. I propose that parish councils should also investigate, reflect, and propose conclusions. When they do so, they are helping their pastors to promote pastoral activity in a very concrete way. They are doing the work of pastoral planning.

In order to show how councils can assist their pastors with pastoral planning, let me tell three stories. They show how Fathers Harrington, Orpila, and Parise have benefited from parish pastoral councils.

The Problem in Father Harrington's Parish

Father Harrington has great trust in his council, whose members have proven themselves by their hard work, discretion, and prudent advice. But when I spoke with him last month, he said he had a problem that he was reluctant to discuss with his councillors. His story is a complicated one, but worth telling.

Father Harrington (not his real name) is the pastor of a large, suburban parish. He believes that Sunday Mass is the one time each week in which he truly connects with the majority of his parishioners. He works hard, with the help of a lay volunteer who serves as director of liturgy, to make the 11:00 Mass dramatic and festive. At this Mass, the choir stands out. Under a gifted part-time conductor, the choir has grown in two years from twenty to seventy voices. The conductor rehearses the choir thoroughly and makes sure that it does not over-commit itself. If the choir sings on Ash Wednesday, for example, it will not sing the following Sunday. Usually the choir reinforces the singing of the assembly, accompanying it with four-part harmonies. But occasionally the choir performs choral solos, singing so well that parishioners twist their heads backward to watch. You would think the choir perfect for this parish's "high" Mass.

The emergence of the choir, however, has caused problems. Perhaps due to the choir's growing size and volume, and perhaps due to jealousy of its charismatic conductor, some parish staff members have been critical. The director of religious education claims that the conductor is not a good communicator. The volunteer liturgy director, who is supposed to supervise all aspects of worship (including the music), claims the choir conductor does not know enough about the liturgy. Even Father Harrington is put off by the conductor's unwillingness to have the choir sing twice in a week. In many parishes, we suffer from poor choirs. A good choir can be a headache, too.

Things recently came to a head. The growth of the choir had spurred the conductor to request clerical help, and the parish bulletin advertised a ten-hour-per-week position to hire him an assistant. After interviewing a number of candidates, the conductor recommended four of them as possible assistants, all choir members. That was in early December. After Christmas, the pastor and the conductor went on separate vacations. And while they were gone, the parish business manager hired an assistant, not chosen from among the four choir member-applicants. The business manager hired a member of the liturgy committee, a person close to the liturgy director. The business manager thought this would improve communication between the conductor and the liturgy director. When the conductor returned from Christmas vacation and discovered that his new assistant was not one of the four he had recommended, he angrily resigned.

The Council's Role

The jealousies of parish life do not make a pretty picture. Father Harrington's inner circle of administrators seemed to be wracked by pettiness and envy. Father Harrington was anxious about whether or not he would have any choir whatsoever to sing during the Triduum liturgies. He did not know how to solve his problem. The last thing he wanted to do was to confess the problem in front of the parish council.

The council, however, was just what he needed—and that is what I told him. Father Harrington already knew that his council members are prudent. And he had a problem that required precisely the studious reflection that a good council can provide. First of all, there was the question of the proper role of a choir in the liturgy. I am not talking merely about what the church's liturgical documents say (although a study of those documents is a good thing). I'm talking about the meaning of a volunteer group, like the choir, that unexpectedly emerges in the parish and makes a huge impact. No one could have predicted the impact. But there it is.

Second, the council helped Father Harrington examine the structure of the parish's administration. It seemed odd that a parish volunteer, the liturgy director, was in a supervisory role over a paid employee, the conductor. Supervision is a very difficult task, even for a skillful, full-time manager. It was unrealistic to think that a volunteer who loves the liturgy (but who also holds down a forty-hour position per week) could supervise the work of a parish employee. The pastoral council concluded that it was unwise to give a volunteer duties that, properly speaking, belonged to a full-time administrator. The pastoral council helped Father Harrington reflect on the structure of the parish staff and how it administers the parish. He is now reorganizing the parish staff so that the volunteer liturgy director is not a supervisor. Although Father Harrington lost the charismatic conductor, he may have better luck with the next one.

This gives us a clue about what councils can do. Council members are to apply their best thinking to real problems. Father Harrington was tempted to avoid the question about the choir with his pastoral council. He thought the matter too delicate. But I reminded him about what he told me: his council is a prudent council. Father Harrington did not need to tiptoe around the elephant in the living room. Pastoral elephants are the business of councils. When councils size up the elephant, investigate how he blundered into the living room, ponder whether the front or the back door is his best exit, and brainstorm how to coax him out, they are doing their duty. By asking his council to help him think through events at the parish, Father Harrington was asking it to do what the church envisions councils doing.

Even Inexperienced Councils Can Help

Some may object to the story of Father Harrington, however, on the grounds that only a well-formed council could treat a delicate issue such as the choir. With that objection, I agree. When it comes to delicate pastoral matters, a wise pastor should consult only trusted advisors. Are we to conclude that a new council should not treat serious pastoral topics? Not at all.

Novice councils can treat serious pastoral matters, provided that the pastor leads them carefully and gradually. Even though a council is new and the pastor is just getting to know the members, the council can still make a substantial contribution. Consider the pastoral council of Father Orpila (not his real name). He is a priest who was born in the Philippines and grew up in the U.S. After several years of work in the chancery office, Father Orpila's bishop gave him permission to return to the Philippines as a Maryknoll Associate. He worked on the island of Mindanao, forming small Christian faith communities among the poor.

When he returned to the U.S., Father Orpila became pastor of a parish with a large immigrant population. His dream was to form small faith communities in his parish—small groups of parishioners who would meet regularly to share faith and to perform some Christian service. To this end, he arranged for his parishioners to participate in the Renew program, developed in the Archdiocese of Newark, New Jersey. Renew trains parishioners to host evenings of prayer and reflection in their homes. About fifty percent of Father Orpila's parishioners participated in Renew, which took place over two and a half years. After that, some of the Renew groups continued as small communities that met on their own.

Father Orpila was happy with Renew. A large number of his parishioners had participated, and many of them were staunchly committed to the idea of small communities. Father Orpila hoped that these leaders would maintain their small communities after Renew. But Father Orpila was also aware that a sizable number of active parishioners—people active in the parish's liturgical, catechetical, and social justice ministries—were not planning to continue in small groups. It was not that they were opposed to the idea. But they were dedicated to their existing ministries. They told Father Orpila that ministry groups, not the Renew groups, were their real communities. They preferred to spend their limited time with ministerial groups.

This created some tension with the Renew groups. One of Renew's principal convictions is that a ministerial group (a parish committee, let us say, or the lectors, or the St. Vincent de Paul Society) is not a small Christian community. A small community is mainly about sharing faith and reflecting on the Scriptures, said these leaders. The small community is the whole church in miniature, not just those belonging to this or that ministry. The small community leaders told Father Orpila that he should promote small communities above every other kind of parish involvement. Some leaders even went so far as to propose an ultimatum. They wanted Father Orpila to say that small community membership should be a requirement for anyone wanting to serve in a ministry.

Father Orpila was dedicated, as I said, to small faith communities. He was also aware, however, that not everyone is attracted to them. He wanted to promote them, yes, but he was not sure how. Indeed, he knew that even experts in pastoral theology are divided over the issue of what constitutes a small Christian community. Father Orpila needed to reflect more deeply on this. He turned to his parish pastoral council.

Considering Two Alternatives
Father Orpila's council was inexperienced. But most of the members had

participated in the Renew program, and so had an idea of small Christian communities. Some agreed with what the small community leaders said. They argued that the parish ought to emphasize small communities, because only through communities can the church offer parishioners an intimate experience of church. Others, however, were not persuaded. They saw that people come to an experience of church in a variety of ways, and that ministry-based groups can be as effective as the communities in creating that experience.

Father Orpila asked this new council to focus on this issue. He had the members read two books. One book was entitled *Re-Imagining the Parish*.[4] Written by a Chicago priest, Patrick J. Brennan, it argues that any parish group can be called a community. Community describes even those groups that are primarily ministerial and have no explicit faith-sharing dimension. Another book was by a Detroit pastor, Arthur R. Baranowski.[5] In *Creating Small Faith Communities*, Father Baranowski emphasizes the primacy of faith-sharing groups. He says that people need these groups because parish ministries and activities fail to give people the opportunity to reflect with and support one another.

Father Orpila's council read these two books. They helped the councillors think through the issues more clearly. Eventually, the council took a middle ground. It emphasized the need for small communities, but avoided proposing any ultimatums. It rejected the doctrinaire position that only members of small communities should participate in parish ministries.

Father Orpila found this a great help. Although his council members were new to the council ministry, they were good at study and reflection. By reading the two books, applying them to the parish situation, and drawing practical conclusions, they were able to help Father Orpila clarify his thinking. The council was new, but its efforts were anything but superficial and unimportant. Councillors were grappling with a central problem: how to give parishioners an intimate experience of church. Father Orpila did not know in advance what the council would conclude. But he knew that its goal was essential to the faith of the parish. His story illustrates how councils can help a parish make a journey of faith.

The Task of a Councillor-Disciple

In the examples from Father Harrington and Father Orpila's parishes, we have seen councils do what many councils fail to do. These councils take seriously the church's official documents. They see themselves primarily as groups that study a pastoral matter, reflect on it, and propose practical conclusions. Father Harrington's council faced the issue of how to understand the emergence of the parish choir, and of how to assess its relation to the parish's administrators. Father Orpila's council drew practical conclusions about how to promote small Christian communities. These two councils did not just meet to report about existing parish ministries or to represent parish groups. They were not simply maintaining what is. They were trying to solve a practical problem.

One of the most frequently asked questions is how to recruit council members who can do this kind of work. This is an important question. Thirty years of pastoral council experience have shown that the pastoral council should do more than represent parish ministries and report on their progress. The church's documents suggest that council members are disciples with a specific task. It is the task of investigating, pondering, and drawing practical conclusions. This is one of most important ways that they can help the pastor in fostering parish activity.

How are we to recruit such disciples? My first answer is this: Get specific about the task of the council. This was the tack Father Michael Parise took with his council and described in an article.[6] Father Parise's parish was a large one in the Boston area whose backbone was Italian-American parishioners. It had not had a pastoral council in many years.

Every busy parish puts heavy demands on the pastor. One can imagine, in an Italian-American parish, what the demands on Father Parise might be. There is the Focolare Movement, the Salesians of Don Bosco, the Legion of Mary, the Knights of Columbus, and the Italian American Federation. Each group wants help from the parish. Each group wants the pastor's support. In his article, Father Parise clearly showed that he did not want to alienate parishioners. He wanted to be a good steward of parish resources.

Father Parise needed help in evaluating the parish's groups and programs. He wanted a true picture about how each was contributing to the parish mission. And he wanted advice about how to possibly consolidate old programs, and even to eliminate those that were no longer effective. He felt that a parish pastoral council could help.

To establish a pastoral council, Father Parise developed his own process. It was built upon the process suggested by the pastoral council guidelines in his diocese, and it added refinements recommended by others.[7] He announced a series of three open meetings, and sent personal invitations to all parishioners whom he wanted to consider council membership. At the meetings, he did some general education about the purpose he envisioned for the council. He also did some work in small groups about the church, discipleship, and the personal formation of the pastoral councillor.

At the end of the third meeting, he invited the participants into the sanctuary of the church. There, in a climate of prayer, Father Parise led them through a process of discernment, asking them to nominate and vote for council members. That was how he chose his councillors. By choosing them in an open series of meetings, he defused the fear that the new council was out to close down and destroy beloved parish groups and organizations.

Recruiting the Councillor-Disciple

There are two aspects of Father Parise's process that I want to focus on. First of all, a clear task. The council's main task, I have argued, is to investigate an aspect of the pastoral reality. Father Parise's reality was a busy parish that needed to set priorities. I believe that if pastors want to attract people who are good at examining the pastoral reality and reflecting on it, they have to say so. Pastors should announce what they hope their councils will do, whether it is clarifying the parish's mission, or assessing the repair of the parish plant, or planning to establish a youth ministry. If they are clear about what they want from their councils, they will attract people who can do that job.

Second, the work of the council must make an obvious contribution to the parish. I have visited parishes in which the work of the council is basically to keep one's ear to the ground, watch the buffalo graze, and listen for the rumble of a stampede. Such pastors want nothing from the council but an early-warning system. Councillors are given no specific duties except to keep a weather eye open. Sad to say, this may not attract excellent councillors. It may, however, attract busybodies, gossips, and people with time on their hands—an unattractive prospect. If pastors want to attract intelligent people with a desire to be constructive, then they should offer them an important and challenging task.

There is no great mystery about how to recruit good members. The principles are simple. Have a clear task. Make sure it is important to the parish. Present it in open parish meetings. Allow people to ask questions. And engage them in selecting council members. If parishes do this, they may be surprised at the gifted people who come forward. These are the people who can understand parish consultation and want to make a meaningful contribution.

Conclusion

The examples of Fathers Harrington, Orpila, and Parise are instructive. Father Harrington's experience showed how a pastoral council can make a contribution to a delicate and difficult situation. His parish was hurt by a personnel problem. A volunteer ministry director was supervising a paid parish employee. When relations worsened, the employee resigned. The council helped Father Harrington see that the volunteer was being asked to do something beyond his capacity. Although the clear thinking of the council was not enough to undo the damage that had been done, it suggested some changes that may keep the problem from recurring.

Father Orpila's trouble lay in the understanding of small faith communities. Some parishioners wanted them to be separate from ministerial groups. Other parishioners wanted to transform ministerial groups into small faith communities. Father Orpila's council helped him think through the dilemma. Even though the council was new and inexperienced, the council's study and reflection helped the pastor resolve a thorny disagreement.

Father Parise formed a council to help him prioritize needs at his Italian-American parish. He wanted broad parish participation, and he also wanted a discerning choice. By holding a series of meetings to educate people about the role of the pastoral council, and by selecting a council through a process of discernment, Father Parise achieved both of his goals. He gained a council that was representative and whose members were committed to the work for which he wanted them.

These stories show that councils have a broad scope and that their work can have practical consequences. From administrative matters to questions of pastoral policy, the council can make a strong contribution. Pastoral does not mean more spiritual than practical. It does not mean visionary but inconsequential. Pastoral refers to the practical work of the pastor. It comprises the proclamation of the word, the parish's worship, its care for the community, maintenance of parish facilities, evangelical mission, and promotion of social justice.[8] This is the work of building strong and faithful parishes with the concerted advice of knowledgeable parishioners, the work in which pastoral councils share.

CHAPTER TWO

A Spirituality for Councils

Loughlan Sofield

When on sabbatical in Jerusalem I spent many hours sitting in what is purported to be the "upper room." This is the room where Jesus and the disciples celebrated the Last Supper. There I reflected on the many things that the Scriptures say took place there. For example, in the upper room:

- the disciples engaged in constant prayer;
- they discerned a replacement for Judas;
- the Holy Spirit was promised and descended upon them;
- the Resurrection was proclaimed;
- the Eucharist was instituted;
- the disciples were commissioned and sent forth to proclaim the Good News;
- the "new commandment" was proclaimed and modeled in the washing of the feet by the Lord;
- the disciples were given the power to forgive sins.

This is only a partial list of the profound and sacred moments that transpired when the disciples were gathered with the Lord in the upper room. Many more things must have happened that the Scriptures do not record. Even this short list, I believe, offers a challenging model for what a parish pastoral council can be.

The most effective pastoral council with which I ever worked made a decision to spend at least one-quarter to one-third of every meeting in prayer, reflection, and study. The members shared a common conviction. They were convinced that if they were faithful to this commitment, they would be better prepared to discern God's will. When I asked what they expected a council to be, one member had this response: "I want the council to be an upper room experience." That response has had a profound impact on my work with councils. I too would like to see pastoral councils be "upper room experiences."

Not all council experiences are. I recall one council that was especially ineffective. It was composed of high-powered, type-A business people. They saw themselves as a decision-making body. They were convinced that any time set aside for prayer or reflection detracted from their work. No matter how hard I tried, I could not persuade them to consider the upper room experience. They could not see that it takes time to reach a gospel-based decision—time to reflect on what the gospel, or the person of Jesus revealed in the gospel, is saying to the group.

My experiences with councils have led me to develop three basic convictions about the spirituality of councils. First, the members of parish councils will be successful to the degree that they make personal and corporate spiritual growth a priority. If the actions they take and the decisions they reach do not flow from their relationship with their God, they become just another corporate management group. Second, the major task of parish pastoral planning is to discern prayerfully God's will and God's plan. Third, councils are primarily prayerful, pastoral reflection and planning groups, not corporate bodies of management. In order to explain these basic convictions, let me put them in context.

A Context for Developing a Spirituality for Councils

My convictions grow out of certain beliefs about the parish and about the parish pastoral council. I would like to say a few words about each. The mission of the parish, first of all, is to form and nurture people to be a leaven in society.[1] The parish helps its people to develop an active spirituality. According to this active spirituality, every Christian has four callings. The parish encourages its members to respond to these callings, the callings of holiness, community, mission and ministry, and maturity.[2] When they respond to these callings, they witness to the person of Christ.[3] We recognize them as joyful, life-filled people of hope. They are people of integrity, committed to doing the right things, regardless of the cost. They are generative people who constantly reflect on how they can most effectively use the gifts, talents, and resources that God has given them. The parish helps parishioners recognize who they are: a people of compassion, characterized by a desire for healing and forgiveness. This is the essence, I believe, of the parish's mission.

Within the parish the pastoral council has a special role. It helps the parish achieve its mission and become a community of collaborative ministry. I have four basic beliefs about the pastoral council. Each deserves a comment.

My first belief about the council is that it is a pastoral reflection and planning group. There are a number of essential elements in this description. To begin, the council's emphasis is pastoral, not organizational. The word "pastoral" implies a need to be concerned about only one question. It is the question, "What is God asking of us?" To give an answer implies another element, the element of reflection. Any council not willing to spend a significant amount of time in prayer and reflection cannot discern the will of God. This is not to confuse a council with a prayer group. The council prays in order to do pastoral planning. Pastoral planning leads to planning for action. Thus the council's work entails a pastoral focus, a practice of reflection, and a goal of planning.

My second belief about pastoral councils is that they develop the parish as a "living Christian community." The Canadian Conference of Catholic Bishops published a small but rich document on parish pastoral councils.[4] These bishops described the council as an organization that shares responsibility for developing this living Christian community. A council performs three key roles in this development:

- identifying needs;
- discerning the gifts and resources available;
- establishing the structures necessary for a marriage between the needs and gifts/resources.

This brief document also identifies some characteristics of council spirituality. A council's spirituality must be communal. If the goal of a council is to build a living Christian community, then its spirituality must reflect this communal dimension. The council that discerns the needs of the parish inevitably perceives something important. It perceives the hunger of people for a deep personal relationship with the Lord. This relationship reveals itself in the utilization of gifts for service and ministry. The marriage between needs and gifts is what we call ministry. Spirituality moves us to action. Ultimately, ministry overflows from one's relationship with God into action and ministry.

My third belief about pastoral councils is that they are leadership groups. According to the psychologist Abraham Maslow, the primary role of a leader is to model and challenge. Councils are to convincingly call parishioners to greater holiness. It is incumbent upon the members of the council to develop their own spirituality. Then they can truly model it for others. Then their spirituality challenges others to spiritual growth.

My final belief about councils is that they must be collaborative. Apostolic success is directly related to the commitment to greater collaboration. My vision of collaborative ministry has a strong apostolic dimension. The goal of collaborative ministry is not merely the transformation of the parish but ultimately the transformation of the world. The concept of collaborative ministry has been extremely well developed in *From Words to Deeds: Continuing Reflections on the Role of Women in the Church,* a recent document published by the National Conference of Catholic Bishops (NCCB).[5] If a council desires to grow as a collaborative entity, the members should read, study, and discuss this document.

To sum up, the spirituality of the pastoral council depends on the parish and on the purpose of the council. The fundamental mission of the parish, namely, to nurture and form people to be leaven in society, must start with parishioners. Parish leadership helps all to develop an active spirituality. In expressing this spirituality, they witness to the person of Jesus Christ. The parish, through its members, should reflect Jesus.

Within the parish, the pastoral council has a special role. It is, above all, a pastoral reflection and planning group. The council plays an active role in developing the parish as a living Christian community. Within that community, the council exercises leadership. If it is to lead by example, it must be collaborative. These are my basic beliefs about the parish and the pastoral council. They are the context for my convictions about council spirituality.

A Spirituality for Councils

My understanding of council spirituality is based on certain beliefs about the parish and about pastoral councils. This is not a nice, systematic, well-formed model of spirituality that can be applied to any and every council. Rather, the model identifies some of the key elements in council spirituality. Each council will appropriate the elements as it sees fit. My own understanding of spirituality is rather simple. Spirituality begins in my relationship with God. This relationship affects every aspect of my life. Spirituality expresses that relationship in action.

I invite you and your council to engage in a process of articulating your beliefs. Try to discern the elements of a spirituality that flow from such beliefs. When I reflect on councils, the following seven elements of council spirituality come to the surface:

1. Reflective

2. Shared

3. Fits

4. Affective

5. Incorporates Failure

6. Moves to Compassionate Action

7. Forgiving and Reconciling

In order to explain what I mean by council spirituality, I will say something about each of the seven elements.

1. A Spirituality that is Reflective

A council is a pastoral reflection group. Reflection groups, by their very
nature, need to acquire a reflective attitude. I believe that parishioners
generally live their lives in the midst of chaos. They face the chaos of the
workplace and of public life, as well as the chaos of private life at home.
In the midst of this chaos, the challenge is to develop a prayerfully reflective attitude. Too often in the past, spirituality has been conceived of as
a retreat from chaos. It might be better to conceive of spirituality as an
entering into chaos or an engagement with it. Parker Palmer, a Quaker,
has most clearly and profoundly described the dilemma:

> Contemporary images of what it means to be spiritual tend to value the
> inward search over the outward act, silence over sound, solitude over
> interaction, centeredness and quietude and balance over engagement and
> animation and struggle. If one is called to monastic life, those images can
> be empowering. But if one is called to the world of action, the same
> images can disenfranchise the soul, for they tend to devalue the energies
> of active life rather than encourage us to move with those energies toward
> wholeness.[6]

One element of a spirituality for councils is the development of a prayerfully reflective attitude. They are to develop this in the midst of a most
demanding lifestyle. If they can do this, they will truly witness to parishioners who are hungering and searching for God in the midst of their
chaos.

Friendship with God, like any relationship, requires time to deepen
and nurture the bond of love. This God-human relationship cannot
develop into fullness without a reflective spiritual life. The section on
collaboration in the NCCB document on women reminds the reader that
true collaboration is impossible unless it flows from one's relationship
with God. Such a relationship demands to be nurtured by reflective time.
This means individual and group prayer, time for reflection and faith
sharing, and attentive listening to the Spirit in our midst.[7]

Let us think for a moment about what might be called a new model
of reflection. This model does not withdraw a person from the ordinary
life cycle, but reveals ways to integrate reflection into the ebb and flow

of daily life. Such a model is atypical. Sometimes those invited to speak to council members about spirituality have developed their spirituality almost exclusively in a rarefied atmosphere. They talk as if spirituality were removed from the hustle and bustle of normal daily life. People with this kind of spirituality have difficulty being reflective in the midst of activity and chaos. Most parishioners, on the other hand, have developed their spirituality in an active milieu.

In conducting workshops in parishes, I often ask participants where they pray. Common responses are the bathroom, the bedroom, the automobile, the kitchen, and nature. (One woman told us she had stained glass windows installed in the bathroom.) Unable to remove themselves from the world, these people have developed the skill of reflecting in the midst of hectic situations. How can your council discover methods for doing theological and pastoral reflection in the midst of your daily lifestyles?

2. A Spirituality that is Shared

A council is called to foster the development of the parish as a living Christian community. Its job is to witness what a living Christian community looks like. Therefore, council members should develop a spirituality that contains a shared or communal dimension.

Many councils schedule a brief, perfunctory, structured time of prayer. Councils would benefit greatly from growing beyond this minimalist approach. They should allow adequate time to share faith. They need to ask other questions. Members might ask one another, for example, "When have you been most aware of God in your life?" "Where have you found God in this parish in the last month?" "Who in this parish most reflects Jesus for you?" These questions provide an opportunity for the council members to share the most intimate part of themselves with others. Such sharing almost inevitably leads to a greater sense of community and unity among the members.

Faith sharing is a very profound and mysterious experience. An example stands out in my mind. I was one of a team conducting a workshop on lay ministries. A congregation of men religious requested the workshop for themselves, their staff, and parishioners. The discussion that fol-

lowed the presentation on spirituality was highly theoretical and intellec-
tual. The parishioners were reluctant to enter the discussion. They did not
understand what was being said, and the theological language was unfa-
miliar to them. Then the parishioners were invited to share their experiences of God. The first respondent was a farmer. He described how he
gets on his tractor at daybreak and how he and God "just talk to each
other until sunset." He concluded his sharing by adding, "But that's not
spirituality, is it?" Next, a member of one of the local indigenous tribes
spoke up. For ten minutes she talked about finding God in the land and
in her children. Her deep piety shocked the priests and religious into
silent awe. Whenever I later met participants at that workshop, they
inevitably spoke with deep reverence about the sharing of profound faith
experiences. The act of sharing transformed everyone present.

One characteristic consistently marks successful communal and collaborative apostolic efforts. It is the ability to share faith. To share faith
with another means that I reveal who God is for me and how God's
presence affects my life. Faith sharing can help councils foster the
growth of the parish as a community of service. Such a community, says
Avery Dulles, is "a community of disciples." If the pastoral council is to
become a community of disciples, faith-sharing is essential.

On occasion I have invited council members to engage in faith-sharing. The impact is always profound. The participants tell me that the
experience helped to build or strengthen trust, intimacy, understanding,
acceptance, respect, and bonding. These are all conditions that help in
the growth of the communal dimension of the council.

Many members are initially reluctant to share this most personal
aspect of themselves. Their early formation discouraged such disclosure.
They understood faith as a personal experience. It was not to be shared
with others. I tell them, however, that every experience of God is a gift.
All gifts, St. Paul teaches, are given for the sake of the community and
to extend the reign of God (1 Corinthians 12–13). Experiences of God
are to be shared for the edification of all.

The Conference of Major Superiors of Men conducted research
designed to discover the conditions that help foster the development of
community. The findings have relevance for councils. The Conference

discovered that the most successful communities shared three character-istics. First, they had a common approach to the apostolate; they had dis-cussed their common call, their common mission. Second, they were able to dialogue on a value level; they discussed issues of the heart. Third, they were able to share faith; they trusted one another with the most personal and vulnerable part of themselves, their experiences of God. Councils would do well to imitate this model: to discern a common mission, to dialogue about what is important to them, and to share faith.

3. A Spirituality that Fits the Person

Luke's gospel proclaims that the Kingdom of God is within. If council members wish to find God they must begin with an inward journey. Spiritualities that are indiscriminately imported or maintained beyond the time when they truly nurture us are debilitating. God is being revealed to each person at every moment of his or her life. I encourage council members to discern whether they have acquired a spirituality that fits them where they are. I ask them questions like these:

- Do you have a spirituality that fits you for your gender, as male or female? Are you cognizant of the different ways in which men and women generally relate to God?

- Do you have a spirituality that fits you for your culture? Does an Irishman, or an African-American, or an Hispanic or an Italian find God in the same way?

- Do you have a spirituality that fits you developmentally? Do you, as an adult, continue to try to live out of a spirituality that fit you as a child or adolescent? Are you afraid to let go of a spirituality that was nurturing at one time but now no longer gives life?

- Do you have a spirituality that fits you for the particular circumstances in which you find yourself?

Our God is a God of surprises, being revealed in ways very different from what is expected or has been experienced in the past. A failure to encounter God in a new way precludes growth in one's relationship with God.

Let me offer two examples of developing a spirituality to fit one's unique circumstances. I once knew a holy, dynamic, bold, apostolic priest who was in a leadership position in our national government. I had the privilege of visiting him just before he died. When I asked him how he was doing, he replied, "I don't have a spirituality for dying." He described how he had a spirituality that fit him when he was an activist but he realized that his former spirituality was no longer sustaining him in his present condition. He was a wise man who realized he had to discover the God being revealed in the process of his dying. Another friend of mine had Parkinson's Disease. He pointed at his trembling hand and uttered, "When I can find God here, I'll have found God."

Thomas Merton says, "Many people will not be Saints for the same reason that many poets will not be great poets. They try to write other people's poems and we try to live someone else's sanctity." Truly holy people are the people who discover the God present in their unique reality.

In conducting workshops with councils on the topic of spirituality it is apparent that many people have a spirituality that sustained and nurtured them at an earlier period in their lives. Now they are experiencing a sense of aridity in their relationship with God. That aridity will be transformed into life only when they are able to discover a spirituality that fits them for every aspect of who they are today.

4. A Spirituality that has an Affective Dimension

Bold leaders exhibit a sense of passion. A spirituality for council members must be passionate. Passion exists only when we give ourselves permission to experience the full range of emotions. Perhaps spirituality has not often been associated with passion. Walter Burghardt, a wise and holy Jesuit, links spirituality and passion:

> In our Anglo-Saxon legacy passion is something to be ashamed of. For strong feeling is a sign of weakness. Love, of course, but let not love enrapture you, let it not glow . . . The rock bottom of a living spirituality is a God who touches me, a God I feel.[8]

Burghardt gave a lecture at Georgetown's Woodstock Center reflecting on the eighty years of his life. One of his pearls of wisdom was, "I regret that relatively little attention was given by retreat directors to the role of the senses, to emotion and passion." Council members are encouraged to cultivate a spirituality that allows them to integrate every aspect of their emotional life into their relationship with God.

Psychiatrists offer the image of a "single channel theory." They picture an emotional channel coursing through our bodies, similar to an artery that transports blood. This channel transports all the emotions. When an individual is unable to accept a particular emotion, one that is feared or considered negative, it blocks the capacity to experience the other emotions. Anger, for instance, is often a difficult emotion to accept and integrate into one's relationship with God. Yet, the *Catechism of the Catholic Church* states unequivocally that anger is a morally neutral emotion.[9]

One of the holiest people I know is someone who is able, like the prophets of old, to vent her anger toward God. Because of this capacity to accept and express her anger toward God, she also has a personal, passionate love relationship with God.

5. A Spirituality that Incorporates Failure

Failure is a characteristic of bold people. Council members should be aware that if they act boldly to propel the parish into the future, they are certain to make many mistakes and fail often. Those who never take bold initiatives are usually fearful of failure.

Many people have been reared in a theology and spirituality of perfectionism. They were formed to be perfect, an ideal reinforced by our competitive culture. Success is equated with virtue. Yet, the beloved and saintly Mother Teresa of Calcutta claimed, "We are not called to success. We are called to faithfulness." The holy person remains on the journey in spite of failure, obstacles, resistance, and setbacks. Long before Mother Teresa, another holy, charismatic figure, St. Francis de Sales, taught, "To get up after a fall over and over again is more pleasing to God than if we did not fall."

These two spiritual beacons challenge a spirituality of perfectionism. God is present in failure as well as success. Sometimes a council may discern that a decision, prayerfully made, results in an apparent failure. Willingness to embrace and process the failure may result in discovering the loving God in the apparent void. Journeying boldly into the future demands a spirituality of failure. Perhaps that was what Henri Nouwen was contemplating when he invited us to be "wounded healers." The Lord is as present, and sometimes more present, in failure and woundedness than in success and wholeness. A spirituality of failure proceeds from an assumption that God is in everything. Those who are willing to explore woundedness, brokenness, and failure encounter a more complete and loving God.

One very insightful friend was asked what he would do if he were in charge of a program preparing people for ministry. He responded, "I would create a program in which they felt free to fail."

In today's culture failure is often inextricably woven together with self-esteem. People fear failure because of the effect it will have on their self-esteem. When perfectionists become aware of their limitations, they compensate by becoming critical or judgmental toward others and life in general. Council members who do not develop a spirituality of failure will often find themselves more competitive than collaborative. Competition is a serious detriment to discerning and fostering God's will.

One solution is to help people move from a spirituality of perfectionism to a spirituality of failure. They need to know that they are good, spiritual people even when they fail. They need to hear that God can be found in failure perhaps more easily than in success.

Jesus is the model for all spirituality, yet his life can be seen as a series of apparent human failures. St. Paul wrote about his own failures, how he often did the things he did not want to do. His life demonstrates how willingness to accept failure constructively can lead to new depths of spirituality.

6. A Spirituality that Moves to Compassionate Action

Being a member of a parish pastoral council is a kind of ministry. The essence of a spirituality for ministry is that it is compassionate. Spirituality and ministry converge in acts of compassion. Compassion is ultimately the major criterion for determining one's growth in the spiritual life. St. Teresa of Avila counseled that there is only one true crucible for testing prayer: compassion. To discover whether or not one is truly praying and growing in holiness, all that is required is to evaluate one's actions. Are they becoming more compassionate?

In a document on young adult ministry, the bishops of the United States flesh out the concept of compassion. The document describes the forms that compassion takes in daily life:

> The journey toward holiness is the path towards finding and satisfying our hunger for meaning, making something worthwhile out of our lives. It urges us to reach beyond ourselves in service to our families and other relationships, to our work, to our communities and to our church, to be zealous in the pursuit of justice for the poor, the marginalized, the unborn, the elderly, the suffering, and the brokenhearted.[10]

Jesus is the exemplar of compassion. Throughout the gospels he responds compassionately to everyone in need. He challenges his followers to "be compassionate as your heavenly Father is compassionate" (Lk 6:36). A truly Christlike spirituality must be characterized by compassionate action.

James Fenhagen describes compassion as "love empowered by holiness." He shows clearly the relationship between compassion and holiness. "Compassion is in itself an expression of holiness," he writes. "Holiness is the fruit of compassion."[11]

One psychiatric dictionary defines sympathy as the ability to feel what another feels. But empathy is more than the ability to feel. The dictionary says that empathy also uses the intellect to think about what it must be like for the other. So sympathy is reserved to feelings while empathy employs two faculties, feeling and thinking. Compassion is not included in the psychiatric dictionary. Webster's Third New International Dictionary defines compassion as "a spiritual consciousness of the personal tragedy of another and selfless tenderness directed toward it." Clearly, then, compassion requires the ability to move beyond feeling and thinking to action. It involves an act of the will. Webster's also refers to compassion as a "spiritual consciousness." It flows from the depths of one's relationship with God.

Compassion, then, is a most difficult act of the will. McNeill, Morrison, and Nouwen indicate why it is difficult:

> It is important...to recognize that suffering is not something we desire or to which we are attracted. On the contrary, it is something we want to avoid at all costs. Therefore, compassion is not among our natural responses.[12]

Compassion not only conveys an understanding of another's pain or suffering, but reaches out to alleviate that suffering. This type of response stems from an experience of God's love. It springs from a decision to express that love in action. Through compassionate action ministry becomes the embodiment of spirituality.

It is interesting to note the frequency with which the word compassion is used today. Perhaps because today's society is highly technological and depersonalized, compassion is emerging as a profound need. A need is something so vital that unless it is met a person becomes sick or dies. The death can be an emotional, spiritual, and, sometimes, physical one. The world contains many people who are emotionally, spiritually, or physically sick and dying because they do not experience compassion from others. Since ministry is the intentional response to a need, then a true spirituality expresses itself in compassionate responses to these people.

"When have you felt ministered to?" That is a question I frequently pose in parish workshops. The most common response is that people feel ministered to when there has been a compassionate response. One man shared his experience after the death of a child. While many friends offered advice, the ones who helped him the most were those whose physical presence and verbal consolation expressed compassion. These friends conveyed their actual presence with him in suffering. McNeill, Morrison, and Nouwen put it this way:

> What really counts is that in moments of pain and suffering someone stays with us. More important than any particular action or word of advice is the simple presence of someone who cares.[13]

Truly Christlike compassion is not selective but universal in its expression. Jesus reached out to everyone. Our response as Christians cannot be limited but should extend to anyone we encounter. The author of an article in the Hindustan Times Sunday Magazine interviewed beggars, outcasts in Indian society, asking them if they recalled any acts of human kindness. One beggar responded:

> In my eight years of begging, I can recall only one instance of real compassion. I was ill and sitting on a *patri* (a low wooden stool) outside the town hall. I hadn't eaten for several days. I sat crouched up in my *durry* (carpet), sobs of grief racking my body. A *sardar* (Sikh) walked past me. He stopped and came back. He didn't say anything. He just led me to a teashop, bought me some buns and tea. We sat together silently. Then he walked away into the night.

Each day presents the challenge to discover those who need our compassion—in the home, in the workplace, in the parish, and in the neighborhood. Who are the "beggars" that we pass each day? Reflecting on the impersonality that seems to characterize our present society, I believe that nothing is more needed than the bold response of compassion.

7. *A Spirituality that Reflects Forgiveness and Reconciliation*

The conclusion of the Notre Dame study on parish life[14] warns that the absence of conflict in a parish can be more a sign of *rigor mortis* than of vitality and community. Anger, hostility, and conflict are inevitable in the Christian community. This has been true from the very foundation of the church until this present moment. It is not the absence of anger, hostility, or conflict that characterizes the Christian church, but the presence of forgiveness and the attempts at reconciliation.

If parishes are to experience a sense of healing and unity, then forgiveness and reconciliation must exist. Anger, conflict, and hostility will not only continue among the parishioners but also among the council members. One of the roles of the council, responsible for fostering a living Christian community, is to witness to what this community should be. Any community, including a pastoral council, should be encouraged to develop a spirituality of forgiveness.

> In a world of flawed communication, community is possible only through understanding others. In a world of painful alienation, community is cre-

ated by accepting others. In a world of broken trust, community is sustained by forgiveness.[15]

There is a difference between forgiveness and reconciliation that some recent writings tend to blur. Forgiveness is an act of the will. Each person has complete control over whether or not they will forgive. Reconciliation demands a response of the other. All anyone can do is attempt reconciliation. No one has the power to force reconciliation when the other refuses it.

Bishop Anthony Pilla, in his presidential address to the General Meeting of the National Conference of Catholic Bishops in November 1997, declared that "a spirit of reconciliation is . . . the essence of our being Christ's disciples and our ability to carry out the mission which the Lord gave into our care." His words could be addressed directly to any council: the essence of their discipleship and their effectiveness in mission is dependent on their willingness to be instruments of reconciliation. Bishop Pilla raised a question for his fellow bishops that could serve as an examination of conscience for any council. "Do we truly manifest a spirit of reconciliation and unity among ourselves which inspires our people and which is necessary if the Church . . . is to fulfill its evangelical mission?"

Forgiveness has the greatest potential to transform a community. However, forgiveness is never an easy virtue to acquire. The normal human reaction is to hold on to anger and resentment and to withhold forgiveness. Doing so, however, is self-destructive. It is also detrimental to mission. One of the major obstacles to achieving a spirituality of forgiveness is the absence of models in one's life. It is to be hoped that the council will model for the rest of the community what a spirituality of forgiveness looks like.

Conclusion

The elements of council spirituality stem from three basic convictions. The first is about spiritual growth. Spiritual growth is not primarily about withdrawal from the world. Rather, spiritual growth must fit our situation in the world, encompass every dimension of our lives, move us to compassion, and help us to forgive and reconcile. My second conviction is about the council's proper work of spiritual discernment. This discernment is shared. It is collaborative, it accepts the possibility of failure, and it tries to learn from it. My third conviction is that councils are to reflect and plan for the parish. Their task is not to manage it like a corporation. Reflection and planning take time. If councils are to deepen their spirituality, they must take that time.

In my reflections I have simply tried to share with you some of my beliefs about the possible elements of council spirituality. Whether you agree with my conclusions or not is irrelevant. What I hope is that you would engage in the same process that I did. Raise your beliefs about parish and parish councils to consciousness. Then, from that experience, identify what you believe to be the major elements of those beliefs. These are the elements that ought to shape your relationship with God and your activity for extending the reign of God.

PART II

Involving the
Right People

CHAPTER THREE

Involving the Right People: Selecting Parish Pastoral Council Members

Marian Schwab

The first time Mary Johnson was invited to consider serving on the pastoral council of her parish her reaction was, "Not me. I don't know a thing about it." This is all too often the response to that invitation. It is so common, in fact, that some councils feel that their most difficult task is recruiting new people to replace retiring members.

It doesn't have to be that way. Serving on a pastoral council can be a satisfying and meaningful experience. When the parish has a workable process of identifying the right people to serve on the council plus an effective process of inviting them, good people will be happy to serve.

Identifying the Right People

Who are the right people for a parish's pastoral council? On the face of it, the question doesn't seem hard to answer. One diocesan staff person gave a simple, practical answer: "They should be cooperative, forward-thinking, and open-minded." An experienced pastor, asked the same question, gave a more poetic answer: "They should be people of wisdom and imagination."

General Principles

The question of the right people for a council can really be answered well only when the concrete situation of a particular parish is considered. Yet, despite the importance of attending to the uniqueness of a parish's council, certain general principles apply to all councils and their members.

Council members should always be people able to act intentionally within a framework of faith. No matter how the council functions, it is there to serve a community of believers with a specific faith tradition. Council members have to understand deeply that the parish exists for the mission of Christ. It is not enough that council members individually be persons of faith or prayer or pious devotion.

Using the mission of Jesus—the mission of the church—as a framework for reflection and decision making about the parish is usually a new experience for council members. Many Catholic adults aren't accustomed to articulating anything specific about the mission of the church. Yet, because the council is enacting a role of leadership within the church, that mission has to be an explicit framework for council deliberations.

Candidates with experience in corporate decision making, or local community politics, may have many skills useful to a council member. Others in the parish may affirm these skills and experience, regarding them as an obvious choice for council membership. That familiarity with decision making in other contexts, however, may interfere with an ability to make recommendations on the basis of the mission of the church.

Commitment to principles like efficiency and cost effectiveness can be second nature to business people. Such members can be startled by the notion of using church teaching about global solidarity, economic justice, or the preferential option for the poor as important criteria for their recommendations.

In others, assumptions about democratic processes of majority rule and political coalitions can be ingrained. Sensitivity to those without power in the community can be a challenge for some individuals. Council members have to be able to understand all elements of parish life within a religious framework. The right people for the council are those willing to make the mission of Jesus the bottom-line consideration in all their deliberations.

Diocesan Guidelines

Diocesan norms and guidelines for parish pastoral councils are essential. These lay out expectations of the local church and can reflect significant dimensions of parishes or councils in the territory included in that diocese.

One set of diocesan norms might state as a requirement that candidates be committed to unifying and reconciling the whole parish and wider community. Another might express the expectation that candidates be willing to work at breaking down parochialism or competition between parishes. Such statements stipulate not only what is valued in that local church, but imply challenging tasks for the council.

Through their norms and guidelines, some dioceses communicate an expectation that council members will be enablers of the involvement of other parishioners—or be change agents, stating that the council is the primary direction-setting group in the parish. Other dioceses expect a much less proactive and more reactive role for council members, asking them to function primarily as a sounding board for the pastor in pastoral matters.

Differences like these in diocesan expectations make a tremendous difference in how the work of the council is implemented as well as in the skills and attitudes needed of candidates. To a great degree, diocesan expectations form a context, shaping the expectations of pastors and councils about what is appropriate in the local church.

Diocesan guidelines throughout the country set norms for council members, naming the desirable qualities they should demonstrate. These lists of norms typically cover categories like these:

- *spirituality*—a commitment to prayer, gospel values, and personal holiness; or a believing, praying, Catholic Christian;

- *knowledge*—of the mission of Jesus, the mission of the church, the nature of the parish, the parish's ministries and people; of their own role as servants of the people of the parish;

- *skills*—in group process, communication and collaboration; skill in listening, in planning, in problem solving and decision making;

- *attitudes*—willingness to speak as well as to listen; openness to other people's opinions; willingness to study church and parish issues; willingness to let go of personal agendas for the good of the whole;

- *ability*—to work with others, to follow through on tasks, to devote required time to the work.

In Chapter Seven John Flaherty gives another list of desirable qualities for pastoral council members.

While these criteria are helpful, they are not sufficient to answer the question of the right people. Thinking about the concrete work of the council sharpens the question. From the perspective of the work of the council, the "right people" are the people who can do the job. In addition, an individual's "rightness for the job" is also affected by such factors as how their personal gifts fit together, how the job of council members is understood in the parish, and how the specific parish context shapes their work. Each of these points should be considered more fully.

The Work of a Parish Pastoral Council

Some diocesan norms refer to *ex officio* members of the council. In some dioceses, parish staff members may be appointed to the council by the pastor or may serve automatically by virtue of their position. Ideally, the participation of such staff members helps the council do its work more effectively by bringing into consideration the perspective shaped by day-to-day contact with parishioners.

What is the work of a parish pastoral council? The *Code of Canon Law* speaks of pastoral councils only in general terms. Canon 536 (about parish pastoral councils) says they are to assist the pastor in fostering pastoral activity. Canon 511 (about diocesan pastoral councils) states that they investigate all that pertains to pastoral work, ponder issues, and propose practical solutions. In line with such canons and other church documents, the work of councils can be summarized this way: pastoral councils should assist in fostering pastoral activity by studying and reflecting on matters of pastoral importance and then recommending practical ways to address them.

In the United States, the work of councils is often described as pastoral planning. Planning may include a variety of activities such as clarifying the parish's mission, assessing needs, dialoguing with ministry leaders, reflecting on the movement of the Holy Spirit in the community, recommending goals for the parish, and monitoring progress on those goals.

In addition, a council is likely to be involved in communicating with parishioners in giving gospel-based advice and counsel to the pastor and pastoral staff, and in working with the finance council to determine how parish resources should best be used for the good of the parish. Because of the breadth of council work, the concrete activities of one council can be very different from those of another.

When the work of the council is seen in concrete terms, particular skills needed by members become clear. Even simple skills, like the ability to bring humor to a tense situation, can be vital to the healthy operation of a council. Fortunately, each council member does not require a great array of talents. All members must, however, be able to operate as a team, with their various skills complementing one another into a productive whole.

All members should approach council service with an open mind and a willingness to serve. No member should bring a mind-set that interferes with the working of the council. Working on a council means learning as you go, so a certain amount of humility is in order. Those convinced that they have nothing to learn are likely to have difficulty relating to the work of the council and to cause difficulties for other council members.

Prospective council members must not be rigid in their attitudes, not biased against any segments of the community, and not antagonistic about contemporary church teaching or the idea of change in the church. They must be patient with the deliberate pace of council proceedings and with spending time in prayer as the council tries to hear the call of God for the parish community.

The Pastor, the Cultural Mix, and Parish Structures

The right people to serve on the council are people who can deal effectively with the concrete set of circumstances the council faces. Each parish is unique in all the world, with a history, composition, and leadership unlike any other. Each of the factors that combine to make up the concrete identity of the parish can affect who the right people are for the council. Because council members operate within a specific context, choosing members wisely requires attention to major elements of this setting, including the pastor himself, the cultural and ethnic mix of the parish, and the organization of parish structures.

The Role of the Pastor

The pastor is primary among the factors determining the effectiveness of the council. Every one of his personal characteristics can come into play as he consults with the council. His attitudes—about collaborating with others in the pastoral care and leadership of the parish, about the role of the laity in ministry and leadership, about the appropriate place of women in the church—all can affect tremendously the work the council actually does and how it really functions.

Other influences on the work of the council can be the pastor's age and health, his personal experiences as a pastor, his ability to think in terms of systems, his vision of the parish in mission and ministry, and his skills in parish management. Added to these are other factors, such as the pastor's creativity, his spirituality, his feelings toward change, and his ability to deal with conflict on the council or in the parish at large.

When the pastor is from a different country than the parishioners—an increasingly common experience in the United States as the number of priests continues to decline—cultural differences may also play a role.

The pastor's attitudes and assumptions, shaped by the culture of his country of origin, may come into conflict with assumptions of parishioners, including those on the council.

The bishop has entrusted the pastor with the pastoral care of this faith community, naming him as its shepherd. Because the pastor is so important, part of the answer to the "right people" question is directly related to an ability to work effectively with the pastor—not a pastor in the abstract, but this particular, real-life pastor, with his unique personality, his attitudes, gifts, and limitations.

The Cultural and Ethnic Mix of the Parish

Another major reality affecting who the right people are for the council is the cultural and ethnic mix of the parish. Chapter Ten deals in depth with this aspect of the council. The important point here is that everyone on the council be empowered to participate actively in the work of discerning God's call to the parish to move forward in mission and be committed to making this possible for others. All members must invest themselves patiently in working toward unity in diversity for the sake of the kingdom of God.

Organization of Parish Structures

In addition to the two major factors named so far—the pastor and the cultural mix of the parish—a third factor deserves attention: the structure of the parish. The way a parish is organized dramatically affects the work of the council and therefore the question of the right people to serve. Examples of these differences are reflected in

- absence of a resident pastor;
- the need to share a priest with one or more neighboring parishes;
- a special purpose for a parish's existence;
- an unusual moment in the parish's history.

If a parish loses its resident pastor, the work of the council may be shifted tremendously. Throughout the country, the number of parish linkages and parish clusters is growing. Along with these linkages come experiments such as cluster councils, where council members might be asked to collaborate with council members from other parishes. (For more on cluster councils, see Chapter Nine.)

Today, increasing numbers of parishes share priests who distribute their time among several communities, with or without the assistance of a pastoral team. Other parishes have deacons, laypersons, or religious as formally appointed pastoral leaders. These parishes would not have a pastoral council as envisioned in canons 517 and 532 but they may have a planning advisory group. Identifying the right people to serve on such a group involves finding people who can work effectively with existing leaders and within the existing, often challenging, structural arrangements.

The particular identity of a parish may require special knowledge, experience, and attitudes of council members. Some parishes serve a special purpose or population, like a university campus, a military base, or a particular ethnic or immigrant group. In such parishes, members of the council might need certain language skills, or an understanding of university or military operations, or appreciation for the spirituality, traditions, and worship style of a particular cultural group.

The specific moment in a parish's history might also modify the requirements for effective pastoral council members. A parish created from the merging of two or more other parishes may call for council members with particular skills, talents, and insights. A parish under severe financial pressure, a parish facing a school closing, or a parish recovering from a traumatic event may demand sensitivities that would not be needed under other circumstances.

In summary, multiple issues affect the question of the right people for the council of a particular parish. Council members must be able

- to relate effectively to the pastor;
- to work sensitively with cultural and ethnic challenges; and
- to cope with the challenge of change.

Preparation for Recruitment

Councils should make a realistic assessment of their distinctive parish circumstances and parish needs before they start looking for new members. People need this information in order to make a good choice about their willingness to be a candidate for the council in their specific parish.

Councils can discover useful information through an informal council discussion about what surprised current members or what they found most challenging in their work on the council. These collected insights can be translated into terms useful in the recruitment process.

The Pastor's Vision

It is also helpful if the pastor will make explicit his vision of the council and its work. No other factor makes as much difference in the work of the council. Really excellent, generous people can be drawn into council membership only to be needlessly frustrated and antagonized when they discover something very different from what they expected. Their potential contribution can be lost to a parish when, with better preparation, their energy might have been productively channeled elsewhere.

The pastor's vision should be communicated to the parish at large, not just to prospective candidates. If the work of the council is visible to parishioners throughout the year, this happens automatically. Parishioners can interpret a great deal about the pastor's stance through what they see as the council's action or inaction.

On the other hand, parishioners' perceptions might be foggy, inaccurate, or at least divergent from those shared among the pastor and the existing council. Before a process of nominations is undertaken, an effort should be made to communicate with parishioners about how the council operates.

The Importance of the Council

The significance of the work of the council must be made evident to parishioners. Parishioners with energy and talent are unlikely to consider council membership unless they can see that the work of the council really matters.

The parish can promise few rewards to those who contribute their time except for the prospect of doing something worthwhile. Because time is an increasingly precious commodity to most parishioners, they have become more discriminating about their choice to give time. Few people are so moved by the honor of being asked to consider council membership that they will immediately say "yes." However, if work on the council is perceived as meaningful for their lives, and if they feel that their particular talents and insights are really valued, most parishioners will, at least, give the idea a second thought.

Parishes have very different experiences of recruiting for their pastoral councils. Some struggle to find even a few candidates, while others have to sort through many nominees. Excellent people live in every parish but they will hide in the shadows to avoid being drawn into time-consuming and meaningless activity. The perception of council work as significant is the most important factor in recruiting nominees.

Calling Members into Service

After identifying the right people, how are they called into service? Practical measures must be in place so that a pool of potential candidates is established. When the parish goes beyond practical considerations and attends to the deeper religious meaning of "call," prospective council members can respond in faith and say, "Here I am, Lord."

The challenge to see service on the council in terms of faith is critical. Otherwise, as soon as difficulties emerge in their role, their commitment may falter. A vision of council work in relation to the mission of Jesus—as collaboration in the realization of the kingdom of God—makes all the difference. Instead of asking people if they would help the parish (or even the pastor) by serving on the council, recruiters should ask whether prospective candidates would be willing to collaborate with others in helping the parish become an authentic sign of the reign of God. The challenge to the parish, especially to the pastor and current council members, is to work with the Spirit in facilitating this insight. Parishioners who recognize they are "being called" in the religious sense have already begun to appreciate council service as personally meaningful. Their reaction to such an invitation is likely to be very different than if they suspect they are being recruited as a "warm body" to fill an opening.

At the same time as it attends to the religious meaning of "call," the parish should design a practical process for recruiting the "right people." Diocesan norms and many parish council by-laws call for a range of processes that usually include the following elements:

- conduct a *parish-wide educational effort* about the role and importance of the council;

- name an *ad hoc nominating committee* or selection committee; then have the nominating committee pursue a *variety of processes* to surface names of potential candidates;

- invite those nominated to consider the role; then provide them with the information they need to make a good decision about their willingness to be chosen for the council, usually through an information session or *orientation session;*

- conduct a formal *selection process*: election or discernment, or a combination of both;

- communicate and celebrate the results; pay attention to *those not chosen*; and formally incorporate new members.

Parish-wide Education

Every time new people are called to serve on the council, the parish has another opportunity for parish-wide education about the role and importance of the council. Pastoral council norms and guidelines in many dioceses explicitly call for this as the initial stage of recruiting new candidates.

Passing up this stage is a temptation to councils too intent on surfacing the names of candidates. That is short-sighted. Parishioners who would make wonderful council members often take years to decide whether they would be willing to undertake such a role. They need time to consider important issues such as the ages of their children or the future of a ministry in which they are currently carrying leadership. Without a special time annually in which they are reminded about the council, prospective candidates may have nothing to challenge them to ponder their availability.

At the same time, an effort at parish-wide education can greatly facilitate the actual recruitment of new members. Volunteers won't suddenly come forward through this process, but an attitude of openness can be established for the day when individuals are approached one-on-one.

Communication with the parish at large about the role of the council should be general but meaningful. At this stage, the importance of the council for the parish is emphasized and explained. The best candidates will be attracted to a role only if it is presented as substantial.

In addition to Sunday announcements and multiple bulletin inserts, some parishes ask council members to tell ministry groups and parish organizations about their experience of council service. Other parishes use opportunities like an annual parish assembly or a parish pot-luck supper to speak about the council and spark conversation about possible candidates.

Parish education about the council is an important effort. It lays the groundwork for the process to come. It communicates expectations and nudges parishioners into considering the possibility of service on the council.

A Nomination Process

Many parish council by-laws designate a few council members as an *ad hoc* nominating committee to facilitate the process. This group can pursue a variety of processes to generate a list of potential candidates. Sometimes council by-laws specify the processes they are to use. Assuming that a council has some latitude about its options, the following are some processes they might consider.

Parish-wide nominations: The first purpose of the nominating committee is to generate a list of potential candidates. While a nominating committee may be tempted to do this alone, it is far wiser to involve the whole parish in the nominating process. Inviting and even urging parishioners to nominate council members underscores the relationship between the council and the parish at large.

Many parishes publish requirements and desirable qualities of council members in the parish bulletin along with the nomination forms. Even if this method results in few nominations, it has value. Parishioners realize they have been invited to name those they would like to see on the council. This challenges them to think about their relationship to the council and the council's role in the parish.

More names are generated in a process where the nominating committee solicits names from groups of people in the parish. A structured nominating process could be conducted during large gatherings such as a parish assembly, a parish supper, or an organizational meeting.

Smaller gatherings can also be used to surface names. This can be especially effective if done systematically. Ministry team leaders might gather names from team members. Parishes with many small Christian communities can conduct a similar effort.

The nominating committee can also ask the council itself and the pastor to make nominations. In small and medium-sized parishes, council members collectively are likely to know nearly everyone in the parish. Sometimes simply going through parish lists at a council meeting generates many names that might not otherwise be considered. This method can avoid the common problem of considering only those already well-known in the parish.

Eligibility of Candidates: Some diocesan norms actually say that those considered for the council should be people involved in some area of ministry in the parish. This probably reflects an assumption that these people know the parish well. This perspective has value. Those who carry leadership for major areas of ministry, however, are likely to face a time crunch if they take on additional tasks associated with council service. Absences from council meetings and lack of time to carry through on responsibilities cannot be excused on the basis of over-involvement in other areas of parish life. People recruited for service on the council must have the time to do it.

The best people for the council may be already heavily involved in ministry. They should not be passed over simply on that basis. They might be asked if they would be open to the possibility of service on the condition that major responsibilities for ministry would be passed on temporarily to someone else.

Some parishes require that council members not be coordinators of areas of parish ministry while they serve on the council. One consideration is the demands on their time. Council members should not have to choose between presence at council meetings and events or involvement in a ministry for which they have responsibility. The possibility of special interest advocacy is another consideration.

This does not mean that council members must abandon all ministry involvement except for their council work. Many ministry roles, like those at Sunday liturgy or monthly work at the food bank, demand relatively little investment of time. The important question is whether council work can be a priority for members to fill their role effectively.

Another extreme is people who clearly have the time to serve on the council because they are not involved in any other parish activities. Rarely is a position on the pastoral council a good first involvement. Neither is council involvement usually a good idea for newly initiated Catholics. People who have recently experienced RCIA may be full of enthusiasm and the desire to participate. They may need more experience with the parish, however, to be able to weather the storms involved in church life without becoming scandalized or alienated. Care should be taken both with recently received Catholics and those new to active participation in parish life to affirm their generosity and to steer them in the direction of more appropriate involvement.

Helping the Nominees Through Discernment: Once candidates have been asked to consider the role, they must be provided with enough information to make a wise decision about their availability. Some parishes ask members of the nominating committee to talk with each candidate in person. Others formally interview candidates. More often, the pastor sends a letter to all candidates, congratulating them on their nomination and inviting them to an information/orientation session.

Formal gatherings of candidates for information sharing and orientation have become common throughout the country. These are often mandated by diocesan norms. Whether mandated or not, common sense points to the value of drawing people together to discuss the issues involved in council service and to have their questions answered. In addition, potential members can meet existing members and experience the style of council meetings.

An orientation session can also function as the first stage in the selection of members. As many as two-thirds of those receiving letters from the pastor will choose to withdraw their candidacy by not appearing at the orientation session. That does not mean that the process up to this point has been a waste of time and effort. Those who received the letter have been affirmed by the recognition of the parish and are more likely to consider a role on the council in the future.

The council should celebrate the presence of those who choose to attend the orientation session and not worry because some withdraw. Elements commonly included in an orientation session include these:

- prayer in a style used at council meetings;

- review of the parish mission statement, and an overview of the work of the council for the coming year;

- clarification of the structure and operation of the council, including the council's relationship to the pastor, explanation of terms of membership, and expectations of members;

- a description of the relationship of the council to parish ministries, to other parish bodies, including the finance council and the parish school board, and to diocesan bodies;

- clarification of the stages of the selection process still to come.

The orientation session is the main opportunity for speaking honestly to candidates about how much time and work council membership demands. Minimizing the time required, in an effort not to discourage people, is a recipe for future problems. Only the candidates can assess whether or not they have enough time for council service. Family and work responsibilities are even more important considerations than involvement in parish life. Current council members help the candidates think through these issues.

Small-group processes incorporated into the orientation session can help potential members discern the appropriateness of this role at this moment in their lives. Time is not the only issue of concern. Other questions, like family support, can also be important.

Often an orientation session includes some kind of process aimed at paring down the number of candidates, especially if there are more willing candidates than positions on the ballot. Having been engaged in supportive dialogue and provided with all necessary information, potential candidates reflect and pray with existing council members for Spirit-filled insight into which names should be considered in the final selection process.

Selection of Members

Most frequently parishes make the final choice for council members by means of an election by ballot. An election process may allow parishioners to speak and be heard on the subject of whom they want to represent their interests. An election process may involve the entire parish or it may involve a smaller group within the parish. Diocesan norms and parish council by-laws would describe the process.

In the past, parish elections for council membership were often pursued in a competitive and superficial way, sometimes disparagingly called "popularity contests." This experience gave rise to criticism of the whole election process as secular, political, and inappropriate for a faith community. This criticism seems to have less basis when the parish election process is supported by parish-wide education, thoughtful nominations, invitations to prayerful discernment, and supportive dialogue with current council members and the pastor.

Elections can generate a positive spirit among parishioners. Often parishes emphatically choose a parish-wide election because a small, internal process can easily appear to parishioners as a decision by insiders. In dioceses where the reflective nature of the council is emphasized, elections can be viewed as one among many other efforts to ensure that the resulting council meets that criterion.

Participation in the choice of council members has, at least in theory, a benefit in terms of emotional investment. Parishioners who participate in an election are more likely to care about what the council does than are those simply informed of who the new members are.

An alternative process of selection, commonly termed a "discernment process," is valued in some parishes and encouraged in some dioceses. Such a selection process involves persons who know both the parish and the candidates making the selection in the context of prayer and reflection. The outcome in terms of the quality of members chosen, supporters of this process argue, is likely to be higher that when they are chosen by the parish at large. The religious sensitivities attached to discernment processes are clearly of value to a faith community. This can act as a countercultural balance to win/lose political processes.

Recognizing the dangers of election processes pursued thoughtlessly and the value of discernment processes, many parishes successfully combine the two. These parishes use a substantial discernment process to sift through potential candidates to arrive at the list of names placed before parishioners for election.

Post-selection Stabilization

After the selection process the council should pay attention to the emotional reaction of those who were not chosen. People who come through a substantial selection process are vulnerable to feelings of rejection. Ideally, at some point in the discernment process, time should be invested in recognizing that possibility. Asking each candidate to consider an alternative leadership position may counterbalance the sense of rejection.

Preplanning is a benefit to the whole parish. Not only are potential hurt and alienation avoided, the parish gains valuable energy for ministry through the commitment of people whose gifts for leadership are newly affirmed, whether or not they are chosen as council members.

A formal ceremony for newly elected council members helps solidify their commitment and understanding. The *Shorter Book of Blessings*,[1] prepared by the International Commission on English in the Liturgy, contains the "Order for the Blessing of a Parish Council." This blessing may be used at a Sunday liturgy (#1193) or at a smaller gathering. The ritual of blessing the council can be a means of catechesis for the whole parish community.

In this ceremony, council members are called forward and all the assembly is instructed in the role the council plays in parish life. Council members are prayed over by the pastor and the entire assembly, and then blessed by the pastor, or another priest delegated by the pastor.

Conclusion

The second time Mary Johnson was approached by a nominating committee to serve on the parish pastoral council, the committee had done its homework. Because they believed that Mary was a "right person" for the job they talked with her about her qualifications and how they would be applied to the work of the council. They were prepared to answer Mary's questions about the work of the council and what she could expect of council meetings. Mary was nominated, entered the parish discernment process, and was selected to serve on the council.

When members are well chosen, the pastoral council benefits both the parish and the individual members personally. The key to choosing well is identifying the right people and then calling them into service. The right people can be identified only partially by a list of abstract criteria. Attention must also be paid to the needs of the particular parish and the real-life conditions of working in that parish.

Finding the right people for the council is crucial for its effective functioning. Spending the time it takes to recruit well is vitally important. Educating parishioners, stimulating nominations, helping nominees discern their readiness, and enabling parishioners to own the process of selection is critical work for the nominating committee.

During the selection process, the council must keep sight of the deeper meaning of its role and ponder the work it does for the parish and the church as a whole. Council members must remind one another how much their work is shaped by the unique parish community they serve —this community of faith that gives them power. The right people can be called forward and enabled to serve, together walking humbly with their God.

CHAPTER FOUR

Pastoral Planning: Involving the Whole Community

George Wilson

One of the first issues a parish pastoral council should consider when beginning a planning process is who to include in the process. The usual impulse is to limit the number of people involved. Fewer people, the thinking goes, will lead to a more efficient process. That may be a mistake. Often, inviting the whole parish community into the planning process is one of the best ways to assure successful implementation of the final plan.

This chapter explores the question of inviting the whole community into the planning process. The first part of the chapter examines parish life through two theories of organizational systems. The second part of the chapter moves from theory to practice by focusing on several issues that must be dealt with in the planning process itself. The third and final part of the chapter introduces practical ways to engage larger numbers of parishioners in the early stages of planning.

A process of widespread consultation offers several benefits to a parish engaged in developing a pastoral plan. The finished plan itself will be better because parishioners are the people best qualified to articulate their perception of the identity of and vision for the parish. Also, parishioners learn and grow from the insights into parish life developed by the planning process. In the end, a plan that involves many parishioners in its development clarifies the mission of the parish, unifies the parish around a common purpose, and generates energy for implementing the plan.

Planning is an essential role for parish pastoral councils. But planning means different things to different people, depending on past experience and current perspectives of parish life. Sometimes these differences can lead to resistance to planning; other times they can engender resistance to the plan itself. A council that develops a well-crafted plan is disheartened if it encounters apathy or resistance when the plan is presented to the people.

Six Basic Assumptions about Change

Planning is about managing change. Since change is an aspect of all life, no parish can avoid it. While change can sometimes be uncomfortable, it can also be a reflection of growth. Creating a pastoral plan is an effort to anticipate and manage change in an organized way.

Attitudes toward change can exert a huge influence on the parish's efforts in planning. If change is seen as something negative, planning efforts might be directed toward maintaining a *status quo*. If change is seen as a positive sign of growth, planning will reflect that optimism. In fact, assumptions about change color the entire planning process.

 This article reflects six basic assumptions about change:

1. All of reality exhibits a pattern of life, death, and rebirth. The forces of life (growth) and death (breakdown) are always at work in every system or relationship. Part of leadership's responsibility is helping people to let go of negative influences and move on in a positive direction.

2. Change is inevitable. Systems that do not consciously address changing conditions will be at the mercy of the agendas of others.

3. Denying the existence of negative forces is a waste of energy. Naming them is the first step toward diminishing their control. Energy spent keeping something from happening is not available for positive use.

4. Problems multiply faster than leadership can deal with them. A focus on problem solving assures the generation of more problems. Life is not a collection of problems to be solved; it is a mystery unfolding, within which obstacles to human intentions are part of the stuff to be dealt with.

5. Energy used in trying to restore what is breaking down (problem solving) is energy that is not available for building something new. Energy is more productively used in discovering forces for growth and commitment and building on them.

6. Persons are of supreme value. Organizational structures are of value only to the extent that they promote the development of persons and their free commitment to a common mission. That is why organizational development begins with discovering the most deeply held aspirations of the individuals involved and developing structures that will realize those aspirations.

Before beginning a planning process, members of a pastoral council might discuss these assumptions about change. Such a discussion will foster communication among council members, clarifying their reasons for planning, uniting their sense of purpose, and minimizing the risk of future misunderstandings.

Foundations of Planning

Both a parish and a parish pastoral council are, at least on one level, human organizations. Like marriages, they function best when the individuals involved are attuned to the divine partnerships they represent. However, as human organizations, they function better when the members have a shared understanding of organizational dynamics. Just as all marriages, not only troubled ones, can benefit from the insights of those who study the dynamics of marriage, so can parishes and parish councils learn from those who study the dynamics of organizations.

One way to approach parishes as organizations is through systems theories. Systems theories look at the ways an organization grows and develops. They also look at the way energy flows through an organization and how this energy is directed and made productive by the organization.

This part discusses two valuable systems theories for understanding organizational life: Stages of Change in an Organization, and The Empowerment Cycle. Together these theories analyze the underlying processes involved in each step of planning. This is a crucial aspect of effective planning. A council that understands the underlying dynamics is better able to design a process that will capture and harness the participants' energies. A well-designed process improves participants' feelings of belonging, emphasizes their value to the community, and unites their various perspectives into a transcendent vision for the future.

Stages of Change in an Organization
Figure 1, the Stages of Change in an Organization, outlines the way a group of people develops a sense of purpose and commitment to a common mission. This sense of purpose and commitment generates enough

Figure 1

MDI 2000

power in an organization to capture the imaginations and fuel the energies of all the people. This power is coalesced through a process that leads parishioners through the four stages described below.

Stage 1. ***Identity.*** Who are we? This is the question of parish identity. The real energy of a community of people resides in the core of their being. In the earliest stages of planning, people need to express their real experiences of life in the community. This taps the core energy and makes it available to the parish.

Stage 2. ***Mission/Values.*** What is important to us? These are questions of vision. This stage of planning invites parishioners to articulate their hopes and dreams for parish life. They connect their experience of the community with the values that give life meaning. In this stage they can express the vision or mission of the parish.

Stage 3. ***Strategic Choices.*** What will we do? This stage of planning examines options and weighs possibilities in light of the parish mission. The outcome of this stage of planning is the articulation of goals.

Stage 4. ***Operating Methods.*** How will we do it? In the final stage of planning, objectives are designed and plans are made for their implementation. Policies, programs, resources, and structures are developed that will help the parish move forward in a common mission.

Effective planning begins by getting in touch with a community's sense of identity and learning what energizes and moves its members. A planning process has a higher likelihood of success when it begins by inviting many parishioners to consider such questions as: "What makes this parish who we are?" or "What is unique about us?" Stages 1 and 2 are critical because they generate energy and commitment. Effective planning cannot begin with Stages 3 and 4. When parishes have difficulties implementing a plan it is usually because they did not pay enough attention to questions of identity and values.

The identity of a parish can never be fully described. Ultimately it is a place of mystery, of grace, and even occasionally of chaos. At the core of any group of people are ambivalent or ambiguous energies that can never be completely examined. These untamed energies exist in even the healthiest communities. They can never be known fully.

Nevertheless, planners need to invite parishioners to reflect on their identity and mission when they begin a planning process. At the very least, representatives of key parish organizations and ministries should participate in this reflection. They need to discuss questions about their basic Christian life. "What makes our parish what it is?" "What is special about us?" This is where effective planning begins. (Chapter Five, "Appreciative Inquiry: A Powerful Process of Parish Listening and Planning," discusses a process of questioning in further detail.)

The Empowerment Cycle

The Empowerment Cycle (Figure 2) illustrates four phases in decision making. This cycle is operating all of the time in parishes even though

Figure 2

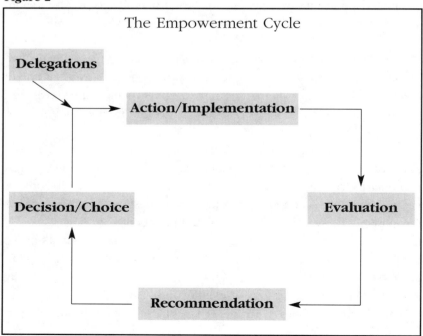

MDI 2000

people are seldom aware of it. Consciously performing the phases of the cycle maximizes the parish's effectiveness.

Today's parishes usually could be described as beehives of activity. However, in a large number of parishes, the pastor or other professional staff often personally direct only the most important activities; much of the day-to-day ministry is performed by volunteers. In the large, and growing, parishes of today and the foreseeable future, this will continue to be the case.

Sadly, a great deal of the energy expended in the day-to-day life of a parish is not efficiently used. Poor communication usually gets the blame. But the real cause lies in an inadequate grasp of the organizational dynamics of community life. The Empowerment Cycle is a way of understanding and managing these dynamics.

Phase I of the empowerment cycle is ***action/implementation***. This phase examines the many activities of parish life: RCIA, religious education, missions, fund-raising events, etc. Planners will find investigating these activities interesting. For example, planners might ask who made the decision to have a parish festival. When was the decision made? What did the parish hope to accomplish with it?

Phase II in the empowerment cycle is ***evaluation***. Evaluation is a natural response to action. In fact, people evaluate all the time. Once I presented the empowerment cycle to a group of teachers. One of them said, "You mean that students evaluate teachers?" Of course. Students have been evaluating teachers since the known history of humanity. What do students do when they register for classes? They say, "What about that course in Physics?" Someone else says, "Oh, don't take him; he's awful; I couldn't learn a thing in his class!"

The empowerment cycle distinguishes between informal and formal evaluation. Evaluation that occurs naturally is called *informal* evaluation. The example cited above is informal evaluation.

Formal evaluation is an intentional process of assessing individuals' experiences within a group. The purpose of formal evaluation is to capture the power of informal evaluation so that the group can learn from its experience. Formal evaluation is central to any planning process. Done well, it generates the energy needed to get past things that did not go well and to build on and enhance success. Parish leaders are responsible for creating opportunities for parishioners to assess their communal life in a formal setting.

Formal evaluation is a way of talking about what is really going on in a parish. It is not about assigning praise or blame. Formal evaluation helps people name their experience. Processes, tools, and exercises that help people articulate their experience and talk about their perceptions in a healthy way are essential to good planning. A plan that fails to build on people's perception of reality is unsound. This chapter will offer several tools to help groups name and discuss their reality.

Phase III in the empowerment cycle is ***recommendation***. This phase involves naming options or possibilities and developing choices for the future.

In this phase the planning group develops a menu of options. For instance, a group looking at the question of stewardship in a parish might develop four recommendations. One recommendation might be to reduce expenses. A second might be to hire consultants. A third recommendation might be to hold fund-raising events. A fourth might be to preach about stewardship. After developing its recommendations, the group would study them and describe the advantages and disadvantages of each. Then it would submit its findings in a report to the pastor, who makes the decision.

Phase IV of the empowerment cycle is ***decision/choice.*** This phase involves weighing the pros and cons of each option before making the choice. Everyone must understand from the beginning of the process who will be making the decisions. The council's job is to develop a menu of good possibilities and complete its recommendation. The pastor makes the final call.

After the decision is made and implemented, the empowerment cycle returns to Phase I, the phase of action. Action now is the implementation of a plan. Parishioners are more confident in a plan that reveals reflection, prayer, discernment, discussion, responsibility, and purpose. They know what they hope to accomplish. Actions that are deliberate and goal-oriented empower people.

These four movements of the empowerment cycle continue even if people are unaware of them. Parishes act, evaluate, recommend, and decide. These phases are informal and less productive until parish leadership formalizes the phases of the cycle, harnessing its power for mission.

A pastoral council can design a planning process that engages the whole community. Such a process takes into account the stages of organizational development put forth by the stages of change in an organization. It begins by getting in touch with the identity of the community and with the vision and most deeply held values of its members. And it assures that the hopes and dreams of parishioners are expressed in the goals and actions recommended by the final plan. An effective planning process also embodies the four phases of the empowerment cycle; it evaluates current realities, recommends ways to address them, focuses on a particular course of action, and outlines action steps to implement the plan. A planning process based on these systems theories helps ensure that the final plan will be enthusiastically embraced.

Facilitating a Planning Process

Involving many people in a planning process often requires the use of a facilitator or facilitators. Many parishes have trained facilitators among their members. Often these people are happy to lend their abilities to the parish for the few weeks required by a planning process. An alternative is for the members of the council themselves to take on the facilitator role. Whether volunteers or members of the council exercise the duties of facilitator, though, all should be required to attend a training session to discuss expectations and come to a common understanding of the role.

Facilitation Basics

In the planning process the whole community seeks the guidance of the Holy Spirit as it plans for the future. Effective facilitators model this attitude of prayer. In fact, the facilitators set the tone of the whole planning process. Their appreciation for the value of the process and patience with it support the community effort. Facilitators respect all participants, express a genuine interest in what they say, and demonstrate sensitivity for their feelings. The tasks of the facilitators are to begin and end meetings on time, to keep meetings moving, to keep participants focused on the issues under discussion, and to assure a climate in which all feel free to participate in the process. Since honest communication is impossible with an overly dominating or too timid facilitator, facilitators must be well prepared to take on this demanding role.

Clarity about Roles

Some council members wrongly assume that the purpose of a pastoral plan is to solve problems. When councillors believe this they may become advocates for one position or another. This can lead to a win/lose confrontation between the council and decision makers. If people work for months on a plan and then someone in leadership shoots it down, they may never want to serve the parish again.

Before beginning a planning process, all participants need to be aware of the roles in a decision-making process. Usually, a council makes recommendations to the pastor, who makes the final decision. This needs to be clear to everyone involved. Figure 3 (page 71) is a worksheet that outlines the roles of all of the people involved in a planning process. It helps planners articulate their expectations at the beginning of the process. This can prevent conflict and hurt feelings as the process moves forward.

Building Trust

All good planning processes are grounded in trust. Trust enables participants to be open and honest with one another. Without trust, participants will be nice and polite, but they will say only what they think those in power want to hear. People are masters of reading signals and making leaders feel good. Unless they trust, they do not always express their convictions honestly.

The basis of trust is a heartfelt belief that the experience of all parishioners is legitimate. Getting to the heart of people's real experience can be challenging to a facilitator of pastoral planning. If the facilitator seeks only superficial, optimistic, or uncritical responses, parishioners who don't agree with those assessments will feel manipulated. Proven tools for building trust are presented later in this chapter. These tools encourage honest expression and can be used effectively by all participants regardless of their level of education or skill.

Before involving the whole parish in pastoral planning, pastors and councils need to answer two questions. The first is the question of

Figure 3

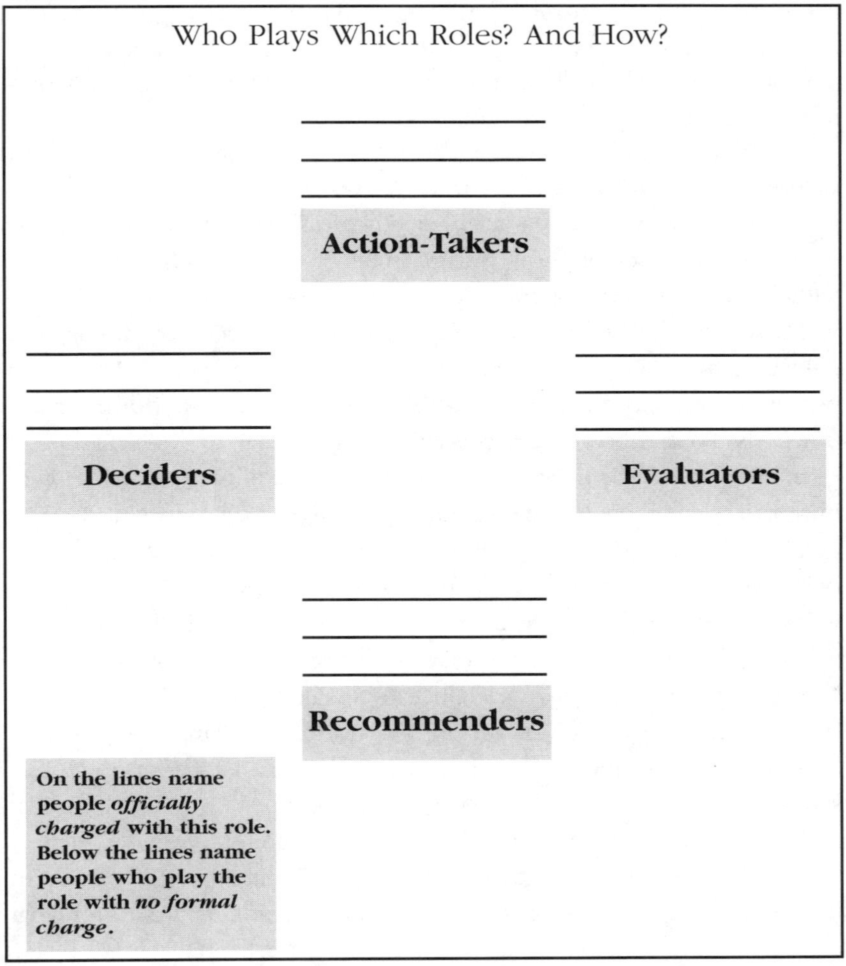

Who Plays Which Roles? And How?

Action-Takers

Deciders

Evaluators

Recommenders

On the lines name people *officially charged* with this role. Below the lines name people who play the role with *no formal charge*.

courage. Are leaders ready to hear what parishioners will tell them? The second is a question of time. Will leaders take the time to make parishioners feel comfortable enough to speak freely? Will they build a trusting environment? If they do not, the planning effort will fail. Parishioners will not tell the truth, and the pastoral plan will be built on an unsound foundation.

Involving the whole community takes courage. In an honest process parish leaders may hear things they do not want to hear. It is not possible to play games with people and earn their trust. If parish leaders do not want to delve into reality, they should not engage in a process of consulting parishioners. This limits the power of the subsequent pastoral plan to engage the parishioners' energies and imaginations, but it protects the leaders from unpleasantness.

Informal and Formal Power in a Group
Every parishioner exercises informal power in the parish. The empowerment cycle describes how the informal power of each individual is gathered into the larger whole. The difference between formal and informal power is this: informal power is exercised by people who are not delegated to play a particular role in the name of the community; formal power is exercised by people who are delegated to perform certain functions. Formal power is accountable to leadership.

Informal power is not a "bad" use of power. People who use power informally can't be held organizationally accountable because they do so outside of formal structures. Informal power is present in every system because formal arrangements do not exhaust people's desire to have an impact on the life of the group. A person who says that "everybody" is upset with the pastor, for instance, is using informal power because "everybody" does not have a chance to speak. Such a person is really speaking only for himself or herself. The use of "we" language gives the impression of greater power. Informal power cannot be stopped; nor should it be. A well-designed planning process strives to make informal power constructive by giving everybody a chance to speak.

Informal power is made constructive by deliberately seeking it as part of the planning process. In the process, all parishioners are asked what they think about certain aspects of parish life. Then, all are asked to reflect on these opinions in light of the parish mission. Finally, all individual opinions are synthesized and transformed into general statements about parish life. This captures the limited power of an individual's judgment about parish life and makes it part of the planning process. An effective pastoral plan gathers the informal power of individuals and formalizes it into group power directed toward a common mission.

Mission

When the stages of change in an organization were described earlier, the importance of the first two stages, identity and mission/values, were emphasized. A parish that develops a vision in harmony with its identity is an effective parish. This parish will be able to draw forth the energy of its parishioners to carry out its mission.

A council facilitating a planning process asks parishioners about the identity of the parish and its vision in order to develop a sense of mission. Mission is different from a mission statement. A parish can have a mission statement that is lovely but does not touch the heart of the community. A lot of time and energy has been spent writing mission statements for parishes that do not have a mission. Likewise, planners may ask about parish strategies (Stage 3) and parish operations (Stage 4) without tapping into what people are really going through and experiencing.

What is mission? Mission is what gives energy. It is a sense of purpose about life. Mission is passion about something people want to accomplish. A clear mission says, "Yes, this is what we will do." It also enables a parish to sort through proposals and reject those things that do not further their agenda. Creating an effective pastoral plan depends on making decisions that are in tune with the parish's sense of identity and mission.

In summary, the council must understand the role of facilitator. Since the council is not determining the pastoral plan on its own, it facilitates a process of gathering the experience of many parishioners. This is a way of discovering and articulating a common sense of the parish's identity and mission. To do this effectively, the facilitator must create a trusting environment. Treating parishioners' opinions with respect convinces them that their opinions matter.

Parishioners are always judging the parish reality. Deliberately gathering these judgments in a systematic way enables the power of informal judgments to be harnessed for the good of all. Roles, trust, power, and mission are critical issues facing the facilitator of a parish planning process.

Tools for Working with Groups

The tools presented here are specifically designed for working with groups in stages 1 and 2 of change in an organization. These tools give people an opportunity to say something about their parish. The tools can be used with large or small numbers of people. If large numbers are present, the facilitator can break the whole group into smaller groups of four or five people. Each small group prepares a report for the whole group.

The best tools for stages 1 and 2 help parishioners tell their own experience in their own words. Using their own language enables people to reveal what is important to them, even when their words are not "church words." Inviting people to use their own words is richer and more powerful than using surveys that ask questions about predetermined categories.

An example of the need to use people's own language comes from an experience I had with a group of priests. I had been in the area for some time, working with the diocese when I sat with a group of priests at lunch. I asked, "Tell me about this place. What do I need to understand?" One man said, "You are never going to understand us if you don't understand the power of the sea. We are a seafaring people. The sea shapes us. We go out to sea day and night, fishing. It can be a tough, grim world of storms and shipwrecks and dramatic rescues." Another priest said, "You used a word this morning that we would never use here. Enthusiastic. People here are not enthusiastic about anything. That's a New Orleans word." The event taught me how important it is to let people talk about themselves in their own language.

Surveys are inappropriate for gathering information about stages 1 and 2 of change. Surveys are always based upon the assumptions of the people making up the survey. Others might not share those assumptions. For instance, one parish surveyed everyone who attended Mass on the First Sunday of Advent. The first question on the survey was, "How often do you attend Mass?" That question contains a whole theology about the obligations of Catholics and the laws of the church. Asking the question forced those surveyed to judge themselves according to the assumptions of those who developed the survey. Questions that suggest people should fit into the assumptions of others make people feel dis-valued and un-empowered.

The facilitator of planning provides a context for people to talk about their parish experience. The first condition that must be stated is, there are no "right" or "wrong" responses. Everyone has a right to his or her perception. Perceptions may differ but each person's view of reality will be respected. The reason for asking for parishioners' input is to discover how they experience the parish and to gather their honest ideas.

Four tools are presented here for helping parishioners express the parish's identity and vision. The first tool is open-ended, eliciting the opinion of parishioners without giving them pre-determined categories. The second is less open-ended, suggesting topics or themes that might be discussed. The third tool helps a parish describe its history and identify important topics for discussion. The final tool helps parishioners express their hopes and dreams and describe the values they want to prevail in planning.

The designers of the planning process should choose the tools they feel are most appropriate for their parish situation. These tools are designed to involve the whole community in the early stages of planning. (Chapter Eight, "How Do We Get There From Here? A Planning Model," shows how these early stages are carried forward in developing the parish's plan.)

Once councils understand the principles behind these tools, they can adjust and refine them to better apply to their own situations. The tools were developed by the Management Design Institute (MDI). If a council copies these tools or gives them to other people, they should credit MDI so people will know where they come from.

First Tool: The Shape of the Community

This exercise invites parishioners to think about the parish in images. The facilitator hands out a sheet of paper with a series of questions on it. The first question is: "When you think of being a member of this parish, what image comes to your mind? Is it like going through fog? Is it like strolling in a field of flowers? Rolling a rock up hill? A peaceful kingdom or battling snakes?" The second question asks: "Who is in the picture?" The next question is: "What is going on? How do people experience events and activities in the community?" The last questions invite parishioners to show where each of them fits into the picture. Other questions can be added to help stimulate thinking.

Parishioners turn the paper over and draw a picture of the way they would symbolically describe the community. The facilitator reminds them that they don't have to be artistic. Their goal is to see what they can capture of their parish system. This part of the exercise should take about 10 minutes.

When the pictures are complete the facilitator invites the groups to analyze them. The following questions may be posed: "What images have people drawn? What common themes emerge out of the drawings? What do the drawings say about the parish community?" This exercise reveals insights about the parish as a system, not the mental state of the participants. Images can capture insights about a system much more powerfully than words can express.

One example of the power of images to clarify parish experience happened when I worked with twelve people in a medium-size city. Each person drew an image that was put up in front of the room. I asked the participants to interpret what the images said. One person said, "Look at that. Every one of our drawings has a symbol of music." Everyone agreed that the music program was the best thing they had going in their parish. Then they realized that they had never acknowledged or celebrated it.

On another occasion I asked diocesan seminarians to make a drawing of the parishes they had served during their intern year. One seminarian drew a circus tent to represent all the beer parties the parish had. In the rectory he drew himself sitting on a Barcalounger watching television with a bowl of little goldfish snacks. Over to the side of the drawing was the church. "All the money goes from the church and the parties to support the school," he said. "The school runs everything." His drawing illustrated a major assessment of the parish. "We say we are here to worship," said the seminarian, "but basically we are here to run a school."

Another seminarian drew a picture of a bright and sunny parish. But there was a cloud over it. The seminarian explained that many good things were going on in the parish, but it had financial difficulties. The cloud represented the question, "Is the bishop going to shut us down?" That issue overshadowed everything in the parish. Parishioners were afraid of their future.

"The Shape of the Community" is an open-ended tool. The value of this kind of tool lies in its power to allow ideas to come from the people rather than guessing beforehand what the themes might be. This exercise lets parishioners tell each other what is important.

Second Tool: "My View of the St. Cajetan Community"

In consulting parishioners about their identity and vision, a pastoral council may not want to use a totally open-ended tool. It may want a tool that defines the focus somewhat. The second tool, "My View of the St. Cajetan Community" (Figure 4, p. 79), provides more focus. It is neither totally open-ended nor does it set up all of the categories. It suggests, in very general terms, themes that parishioners might want to discuss.

This worksheet was developed for a non-parish faith community, a group of adults and families who were attracted to the liturgies at a Franciscan center. When the Franciscans turned the center into a retirement complex, the members of this group decided to continue as a faith community that we will call "St. Cajetan's." Their life is precarious because at any moment the complex could take over the chapel and deny them worship space. Or their priest could retire or die, and they have no guarantee that they could find another one.

At St. Cajetan's they did not want to do an open-ended process because they did not think they had enough time. The committee designing the process developed this tool, which suggests some topics people might want to talk about. This helps people that have trouble dealing with a totally open-ended process but does not constrain them to think only in terms chosen by the committee.

To use this tool the facilitator asks each person to write down three things he or she most wants to talk about. Then the individuals are put into small groups of three or four to discuss their ideas with others.

Following the small group discussion each person is invited to note the things that he or she wants to celebrate about life in the community, to note the things that are of most concern, and to jot down his or her top three dreams and hopes. The tool encourages small group discussions that teach people how others feel about a variety of community issues. It empowers parishioners to create a conversation about things that are important to them.

When the results of the conversations at St. Cajetan's were collated, several themes emerged. First, the people wanted to celebrate the fact that their liturgies were great. Their priest was a wonderful presider who engaged the whole community in worship. Second, they articulated their concerns about their survival as a community. This helped them design steps that they could take to assure their future. Finally, they created task forces to deal with their concerns. The tool sparked a conversation that clarified their situation and suggested ways to deal with it.

Third Tool: "What Was It Like Then? What Is It Like Now?"
Another tool is entitled "What Was it Like Then? What Is it Like Now?" (Figure 5, page 80). This tool also provides categories to think about. Asking, "What were things like when you arrived?" is a way of uncovering the history of the parish and providing a framework for discussing important themes. The facilitator invites participants to reflect on their experience of the parish and to name the things that they think are the most important to talk about.

These tools are crucial in the early stages of parish planning. They help parishioners articulate and share their experience of the parish. This shared experience becomes the source of the identity and mission of the parish. A pastoral plan built upon the parishioners' real experience has a solid and secure base in reality. It will not be a castle in the air.

Fourth Tool: "Mapping Our Future"
Clarifying the identity of the parish is the first stage in the development of the parish as an organization. The next stage of the planning process moves into articulating values. The final tool, shown in Figure 6 (page 83), describes a scenario that helps the group envision the future of the

Figure 4

My View of the St. Cajetan Community

We all have different perspectives on our community, and that's OK. Look over this collection of possible themes to see which ones are most significant from your point of view. Feel free to add one if we missed it.

Ecumenism	Married Couples	Facilities	Community
Catechesis		Liturgy	Worship Space
Inclusion	Social Mission	Music	Finances	Location
Outreach	Demographics	The Marginalized	Persons with Disabilities	Young Adults
Adult Formation	Governance			Children
	Engaged	Spiritual Formation	Family	

Pick three themes that you want to celebrate and give your reason:

_____

Pick three themes that cause you concern or present a challenge for us to consider in our planning

| Theme | Concern or Challenge |

1.
2.
3.

What are your top three dreams/hopes for our community?

1. _____

2. _____

3. _____

1. _____

2. _____

3. _____

Any further observations you want to share with the Planning Committee?

Figure 5

St. Cajetan Catholic Community
What was it like then?
What is it like now?

**When I Came to
St. Cajetan's**

**St. Cajetan's
as I See It Today**

Make-up of
Members

Community Life

Participation

Involvement

Structures

Outreach

Leadership

Worship

Facilities

Other Aspects?

MDI 2000

whole system as a way of discovering and articulating underlying values and assumptions. These assumptions and values determine the criteria to be used in planning for their future.

The "Mapping Our Future" exercise asks parishioners to envision their future. Since some people need time to do this, the exercise is given as homework. The facilitator explains that participants are not expected to create fully finished plans. Rather, the individual efforts will constitute the starting point of a discussion of their assumptions about future realities. In the ensuing discussion they may find that they share some assumptions but not others. Or they may find that some assumptions are more realistic than others.

The "Mapping Our Future" exercise was used in one diocese to plan for the future assignments of priests. The bishop formed a blue-ribbon commission to address the task. In assigning the commission the bishop described the situation this way: "We currently have a certain number of priests. All of the data tell us that ten years from now we will have thirty fewer. I want to make decisions based upon a common vision and criteria that reflect our values as a diocese. I am asking each of you to develop a plan for the deployment of these priests."

Each member of the commission created a plan for the assignment of priests and brought it back to the bishop. One plan described a future in which a parish with 500 members had one priest, a parish with 1000 members had two priests, etc.—larger parishes would receive greater numbers of priests. When the commission looked at this scenario they asked, "Will the assignment of priests be based only on numbers? Is this the understanding of church on which we want to build the future of the diocese?" Another plan showed rural parishes losing priests while the suburbs "gobbled them up." This scenario also provoked a discussion of underlying values.

In the end the diocese articulated a principle that a formal church presence would be maintained in every county in the diocese, even if that meant that the big cities might not have enough priests to staff all of the parishes. "Mapping Our Future" enabled the bishop and his commission to clarify their assumptions, to articulate their values, and to determine the criteria that would be the framework for planning.

Conclusion

This chapter has focused on involving the whole community in the planning process. This involvement is most necessary in the early stages of planning described in Stages of Change in an Organization as the *identity* and *mission/values* stages. Building a plan on the actual, lived experience of parishioners assures that the plan will be realistic and enjoy the support of parishioners. Further, the empowerment cycle shows how including parishioners in the *evaluation* and *recommendation* phases coalesces the informal power of individuals into formal group power for carrying forward the parish mission.

Competent facilitation invites and respects the input of every parishioner in these early stages of planning. Facilitation clarifies roles in planning, establishes trust, empowers everyone, and develops a shared vision of the community. Tools that enable parishioners to honestly express their experience of the parish community and to share their insights with other parishioners are vital to an effective planning process.

The following statements summarize my conclusions on involving the whole community in pastoral planning:

• No plan, however wise its content, will ever be carried out if it does not enjoy the support of the people who are going to be affected by it.

• People will give their support—even to outcomes they would not have proposed themselves—if they experience that the decision-making process genuinely valued their input.

• The tools used to draw out the input of the participants need to respect the organization's developmental processes, moving from identity through definition of mission to strategies and operational methods of carrying out the mission.

• The process used should clearly demarcate the differences between the roles of evaluation, the development of options for choice, the moment of choice itself, and the delegations required for implementing what has been decided.

• The success of any group process depends on the leader's genuine openness to hear the actual lived experience of the members, no matter how poorly they may be able to articulate it.

Figure 6

"Mapping" Our Future
A Personal Worksheet

1. There are presently _____ members in _____ parish. Other information you have received describes the present distribution by geographic location, income, ages, and numbers of family members.

2. By the year _____ we can reasonably anticipate that we will have _____ members.

3. Your task is to propose how the ministry resources of the parish would be deployed if the parish as a whole is to be effective in fulfilling its mission *as you would hope it can be*. Draw your own preferred map.

4. Your "map" can include such things as:

- increasing the level of personnel support to any present ministry
- placing personnel resources in different ministries
- focusing the roles that ministry personnel play in new ways
- initiating **new ventures** and **new models** for carrying out our ministries
- changing the ways we configure our ministries
- withdrawing personnel from existing ministries

5. Before creating your map, try to articulate the **"core idea"** or **focus** or **dominant value** your proposed alignment seeks to achieve.

6. Be prepared to describe the **church context** you foresee "down the road": the realities to which your deployment seeks to respond.

Your "map" must show how our ministries will be supported by realistic resources.

7. **Bring your completed map, including your description of the probable context and the core values, with you to the next meeting. Our individual maps will constitute the starting point of our discussions. Thank you!**

MDI 2000

In short, involving the whole community, especially in the early stages, in developing a pastoral plan is the best way to assure the success of the final plan.

PART III

Doing the Research

CHAPTER FIVE

Appreciative Inquiry: A Powerful Process for Parish Listening and Planning

David DeLambo and Richard Krivanka

When the bishops of Vatican II first proposed the idea of diocesan pastoral councils, they expressed the purpose of such councils in one brief sentence. Pastoral councils, they said, are "to investigate and consider matters relating to pastoral activity and to formulate practical conclusions concerning them." However, while the bishops suggest focusing on pastoral *matters*, many councils focus exclusively on pastoral *problems*—those things that are wrong with the parish. We believe that pastoral matters are essentially about pastoral "life" and what supports and sustains this life. Appreciative Inquiry is a way of reframing the focus of councils, shifting the line of questioning from what is wrong, to what is right and what will enhance life in the parish. In doing so, Appreciative Inquiry generates the creativity, energy, and enthusiasm needed to bring about positive change and vibrant parish life.

When conducting workshops on Appreciative Inquiry, we begin with an exercise. We divide participants into small groups. We give those on the left side of the room this discussion topic:

> Describe a key problem in your parish, something you are especially frustrated with or concerned about. What are some of the key factors that cause this problem?

Those on the right side of the room receive this topic:

> Describe a best moment in your parish, a time when you felt most alive, enthused, or inspired about being a member of your parish. What were some of the things people did which contributed to making this a "best moment" at your parish?

After their discussions we ask them how they feel. Those on the left tend to use words like "negative," "angry," "defensive," and "frustrated," and report "having less energy." Those on the right, however, report "increased energy," "animation," "excitement," and "enthusiasm." The results are always the same.

This exercise shows the impact that a line of questioning can have on people. We asked those on the left a question characteristic of the traditional "problem-solving" approach to planning, patterned on the medical model of inquiry. A parish, like an ailing patient, has a problem. You name the problem (the symptoms), determine the cause (the diagnosis), propose a solution (the prescription), and implement it (the treatment).

We asked those on the right side of the room a question characteristic of Appreciative Inquiry, a life-centered approach to planning. You start by identifying the best, life-giving qualities of a parish, often captured in a "best moment" or a high-point. You then determine how to enhance that life, design a strategy, and carry it through to completion.

In this chapter we define Appreciative Inquiry, look briefly at its spiritual underpinnings, present the organizational principles on which it is based, then walk though the phases of the process, offering ways to implement it in a parish setting.[1]

Appreciative Inquiry: A Definition

To "appreciate" means to value, recognize, or affirm the strengths, successes, and potentials of a person or thing. We appreciate things that give life, health, vitality, and excellence.

To "inquire" is to explore or discover. It is to ask questions with the hope of seeing new potentials and possibilities. Appreciative Inquiry is thus the process of asking questions and exploring things that give life, health, vitality, excellence, and success.[2]

Appreciative Inquiry means more than asking positive questions. Many planning methodologies do this, inquiring about the strengths as well as the weaknesses of a parish. What makes Appreciative Inquiry different is that it makes life, rather than problems, the center of investigation. The entire focus of the process is on what gives and what enhances life.

This method has been developed over the past fifteen years by David L. Cooperrider, Professor of Organizational Behavior at Case Western Reserve University in Cleveland, Ohio. It has been used successfully in a wide variety of organizational settings throughout the world. It is also the primary planning methodology we use in the pastoral planning office of the Diocese of Cleveland.

The Spiritual Underpinnings

We have applied Appreciative Inquiry within the context of Christian faith. Its life-centered focus parallels the words of Jesus found in the Gospel of John: "I came so that they might have life and have it more abundantly" (John 10:10). Appreciative Inquiry helps us find life and experience it more abundantly.

The apostle Paul shares this life-centered focus. In his letter to the Philippians (4:8–9), Paul concludes with this exhortation:

> Finally, my brothers and sisters, whatever is true, whatever is honorable, whatever is just, whatever is pure, whatever is loving, whatever is gracious, if there is any excellence, if there is anything worthy of praise, think

about these things. Keep on doing what you have learned and received and heard and seen in me. Then the God of peace will be with you.

Paul is writing to a community in turmoil. Some in Philippi have turned against him, threatening all that he has accomplished with them. Instead of rebuking or problem solving, Paul advocates a change of focus towards things that give life and hope. He knows the fruits this will have. "The God of peace," he says, "will be with you."

A great gift of Paul to the early church was his ability to see (and help others to see) the goodness and wonder of God at work in every setting. Appreciative Inquiry, like Paul, helps us see the hand of God in all aspects of life.

You also find strains of Appreciative Inquiry in the great mystics of the West. Meister Eckhart, for example, makes explicit the link between the life of faith and the appreciative perspective when he says:

> The [person] who has God essentially present to [him/her] grasps God divinely, and to [him/her] God shines in all things.[3]

Fr. Michael Himes, Professor of Sacramental Theology at Boston College, speaks in a similar vein when describing the sacramental imagination:

> To see anything for what it is, is to see the goodness of it, the love of God for it, God's grace in it. The challenge is to see things as they are, as God sees them. And as God says about creation, "It is good. It is very good." That which is always and everywhere, God's grace, must be noticed, accepted, and celebrated.[4]

We often fail to notice the abundance of God's gifts because we do not pay attention. Appreciative Inquiry fosters attentiveness and helps us see the goodness of God in everything. It combines faith formation with organizational development.

The Five Basic Principles

Appreciative Inquiry works because it is based on sound theoretical principles. These principles, tried and tested, are confirmed in a number of disciplines. Let us look briefly at the principles underlying Appreciative Inquiry.

The Constructionist Principle

In his book *The Seven Habits of Highly Effective People*,[5] Stephen Covey states that we see things not as they are, but as *we* are. In other words, "objective" reality is highly "subjective." It is an interpretation based on the mental maps we carry in our heads. These mental maps are important, says Covey, because the way we *see* shapes our actions (what we *do*), which, in turn, influences the results we *get*. Covey refers to this cycle as the "basic change model" (see Figure 1, below).[6] Change begins when we change the way we see, the way we construct reality.

Psychology validates the Constructionist Principle in what is known as the "Pygmalion Effect." The classic example is the teacher in England who was told by researchers that the children on one side of her classroom were bright, while those on the other were less gifted. These designations, said the researchers, were based on test scores. A couple of days later, the researchers realized they had made a mistake. They had reversed the scores. The children they had said were bright were, in fact, the ones with the lower test scores. The children with the higher test scores were the ones they had labeled less gifted.

Figure 1

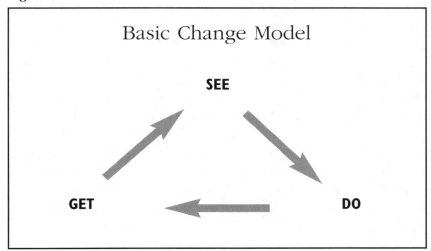

Instead of correcting their mistake, the researchers decided not to tell the teacher, but to wait and see the results. Six months later the children were re-tested. The scores of the children mistakenly identified as bright rose 18 points. The scores of the children mistakenly identified as less gifted dropped 14 points. The effect of the teacher's image of the children was reflected in their test performance.

The implications of the Constructionist Principle for parish planning are clear. If the way we see "constructs" or creates the reality we experience and the results we get, our choice of lens is a fateful act. As we illustrated at the beginning of this chapter, the "problem-solving" lens often leads to negativity, pessimism, and decreased energy for change. The "appreciative" lens leads to energy, optimism, and enthusiasm for change.

The Poetic Principle

Simply stated, organizations are like poems (or even biblical texts): a source of endless interpretative possibilities. Virtually any topic related to human experience can be explored in a parish setting. Why? Because all the "stuff" of life (like creativity, innovation, joy, hope, alienation, stress, anxiety, etc.) exists in every parish. All are possible and valid topics of exploration.

But in assessing a parish situation, we do not always look for the life-giving aspects. And when we do, we often pass over them quickly in our haste to get to the heart of the *problem*. Our society favors the "problem-solving" lens. Our notion of higher-level thinking is "critical" thinking, and is associated with finding weaknesses and flaws. The Poetic Principle challenges this bias, reminding us that the value of a lens lies in what it enables a person to see. When striving to improve the spirit of a parish, we find the appreciative lens, which carefully examines those moments that have brought life, to be a better approach.

We know some are of the opinion that spending time on what is going well is counterproductive. If it's not broken, leave it alone. However, studying what is going well helps a person to understand the conditions for success that made an exceptionally good moment possible. By understanding how those moments came about, a person is in a good position to replicate them and increase their frequency.

The Principle of Simultaneity

We often think of inquiry and organizational change as separate moments—as if the organization is somehow in stasis during the planning process, with change beginning the moment the reorganization has been achieved, the new plan adopted, or the mission statement ratified. In point of fact, change begins the moment you ask the first question. The question and the change are simultaneous. The exercise at the beginning of this chapter (that of describing either a "best moment" or a "key problem") illustrates the power of even one question on participants. Appreciative Inquiry practitioners capture the essence of the Principle of Simultaneity in their maxim, "Inquiry is intervention." There are no neutral questions. The seeds of change are implicit in the first questions we ask. What we seek, we find. What we find, we talk about. What we talk about leads to images that guide us into the future—the material from which the future is conceived and change is made.

The Anticipatory Principle

Kennon Callahan, in *Twelve Keys to an Effective Church*, captures the thrust of the Anticipatory Principle when he writes:

> The watershed question for many people in many congregations is: Do you believe that your best years are behind you, or do you believe that your best years are yet before you? Some churches believe that their best years are behind them. Some people believe that their best years have been. They behave and act as though the future will be less than that which is past. And it is precisely because they behave and act that way that the future for them turns out to *be* less than that which has been. Effective, successful churches live in the confidence of God's promise that some of their best years are yet to come.[7]

Callahan's point is that the image of the future guides the current behavior and ultimate future of a parish. By anticipating the future, we help create it. We must build the foundation of planning on the core images through which the parish expresses its identity. Appreciative Inquiry surfaces these core images through the questions it asks.

The Positive Principle

The momentum for change in a parish requires large amounts of positive affect, social bonding, and creative energy. The old adage that nothing happens between strangers is true. Social bonding enhances collaboration, while positive affect lessens resistance to change. The Positive Principle states that the more positive the questions used to guide community-building or parish planning, the longer lasting and more effective the change will be. Positive questions lead to positive images, which increase positive energy, resulting in positive change.

The power and value of positive images is indisputable. Consider the "placebo effect" in medicine. Medical researchers believe that one-third to two-thirds of the effectiveness of a treatment is the patient's expectation that the treatment will work. Appreciative Inquiry increases the expectation of positive change.

There is a second, similar effect noted in medicine. In Mayo Clinic studies,[8] physicians discovered that the recovery rates of heart surgery patients correlated with their expectations of recovery. Patients who recovered more slowly had about a 1:1 ratio of positive to negative self-talk. That means for every time patients expressed belief that they were getting better, they also expressed belief that they were not. In healthy recoveries, the ratio of positive vs. negative self-talk was about 2:1 or greater. The more positive the patients' self-talk, the more likely they were to experience a successful outcome for their treatment. Appreciative Inquiry creates positive self-talk in a parish, increasing the likelihood that planning will be effective.

Is Appreciative Inquiry Pollyannaish?

Some criticize Appreciative Inquiry as escapist, pollyannaish, a way to avoid unpleasant realities. We believe, however, that Appreciative Inquiry does not avoid problems; it reframes them. When people are upset it is usually because something they cherish or want is not happening. For example, when parishioners complain about overly casual dress at Mass, the real issue is typically that their understanding of reverence (expressed in wearing one's "Sunday Best") is not being valued and respected by others. The deeper issue is the desired life-giving reality or quality, not its absence. Appreciative Inquiry allows people to express what they really want in a more constructive, empowering way.

Appreciative Inquiry in Parish Planning

The planning cycle for Appreciative Inquiry is often called the "4-D" cycle because of the names given to its different phases: Discovery, Dream, Design, and Destiny (see Figure 2).

1. Discovery Phase

The discovery phase is so named because its central task is to "discover" sources of life in the parish, particular moments or events that capture the best of "what is." The guiding question in this phase is "What gives life?" We find this the most important phase of the planning process because it helps parishioners re-image their parish, and their parish experience, in a hope-filled, positive way. In the discovery phase parishioners share stories of exceptional accomplishments, of what first

Figure 2

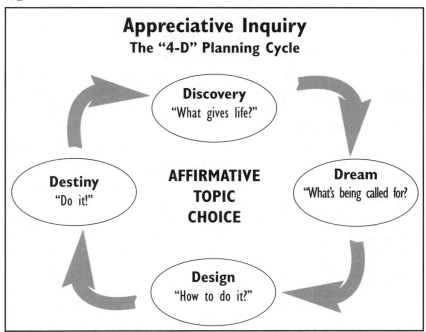

attracted them to the parish and what keeps them there. They share stories of aspects of the parish that they value and what they hope for in
the future. In the discovery phase, there are six initial questions:

1. Parishioners' **beginnings** with the parish:
   What attracted you to this parish? What were your initial impressions
   of the parish? What excited you about the parish?

2. Parishioners' **most life-giving experience** at the parish:
   What was your most life-giving experience with the parish? Recall a
   time when you felt most alive, fulfilled, or enthused about being a
   parishioner. What made it a peak experience for you?

3. Parishioners' **personal values** and what they **most value about the
   parish**:
   Describe something you value deeply about yourself (e.g., as a
   Catholic, a worker, a family member, etc.). What do you value most
   about the parish? What about the parish is most central to you in your
   attachment to it?

4. The **impact of the parish** on the members' lives:
   What is the single most important thing the parish has contributed to
   your life in the past year?

5. The **essential spirit** of the parish:
   What represents the essence of this parish? What is its most life-giving force, without which it would cease to exist?

6. **Images of the future** for the parish:
   If you could enhance or transform this parish in any way you wished,
   what three things would you do to heighten its vitality and overall
   health?[9]

When planning, we generally ask a pilot group of parish leaders (anywhere
from 30 to 80 people) the above questions. Out of their responses, key

sources of life in the parish are identified to serve as the affirmative topics for further inquiry. These topics become the focus for in-depth exploration into "what gives life" and "what can enhance life" in the parish.

We have found that the most powerful way to conduct the discovery phase is through personal interviews. The intimacy of the personal interview enhances the power of the life-giving stories.

Personal interviews take about 45 minutes to an hour. Step one is to train the individual interviewers. This is done in a large group. We walk the group through the questions on the interview protocol and show them how to write up the results of their interviews. Step two is to have them form pairs, with each person taking 45 minutes to do an actual interview with the other person. Step three is to assign the interviewers specific parishioners (randomly selected from the parish roster) to interview. Each interviewer, or two-person team if preferred, interviews three or four parishioners.

To further reflect on the value of the interview even with the time it requires, we want to describe one experience in a large suburban parish where the average annual household income exceeds $100,000. It is fair to say that the parishioners are very busy people, concerned about not wasting time. Many of these people are not available for volunteer work during the week because of business-related travel. Seventy-five interviewers were trained initially on a Sunday afternoon. Each of them then received the names of three or four people to interview.

Later, we called the parish planning team coordinator to arrange the next step. In our conversation, she stated:

> We have had such wonderful interviews. This is such a wonderful parish, but you know, we weren't aware of how blessed we are. I have been an active leader here for years, but I didn't have a clue about what goes on in people's lives here. They come and go and we make assumptions about what is happening with them. But people said such powerful things about what this parish means to them, things that we never knew. If we never did anything more with the interviews—no summary, no strategic plan— the whole process would still have been worthwhile. People are calling and asking us to interview them, and when we finish they ask if they can interview other people.

The enthusiasm generated by Appreciative Inquiry is contagious. It is the only planning methodology we know of that has so much potential to positively change the discourse of a parish. By "discourse" we mean the way that people think and talk about a parish. Discourse that focuses on the things that diminish and frustrate people, on things that take from life rather than add to it, is disabling and paralyzing. Discourse about the way God is working in people's lives empowers parishioners. They become more creative and enthusiastic.

The discovery phase of Appreciative Inquiry is not confined to personal interviews. A group process can also be used in the context of a "town hall" meeting. Those at the meeting are formed into small groups of four to six to discuss appreciative questions. The sharing around each question is recorded by the groups and collected at the end of the meeting. This "town hall" style Appreciative Inquiry is a particularly effective means of soliciting parishioner input when preparing to write a parish mission statement or a statement of core values. Since discussion takes place in a group, it is not possible to explore all six initial questions as you would in a personal interview. Instead, we generally use two questions: the "most life-giving experiences" and "what is most valued about the parish." After the former question is addressed, people are asked at each table to discern the common values embodied in the stories of their "most life-giving experiences," values that reflect who they are and what they stand for as a parish community at their best.

It is also possible to use a written survey *after* the appreciative interviews or town hall meetings have been conducted. The survey can be used to test whether the emerging topics and related ideas that have surfaced are more broadly supported for further exploration and planning. In Appreciative Inquiry, this is called a "consensus validation survey," and it is distributed to the parish at large. We do not recommend using a written survey to explore the six initial questions in the discovery phase. Hearing the story firsthand is more powerful than reading a few sentences on a sheet of paper.

2. Dream Phase
During the dream phase the imagery and data collected in the discovery

Phase is used to paint a compelling picture of a more valued and vital future for the parish. "What is being called for?" is the guiding question. During the Dream Phase, a parish that does not already have a mission statement can create one. Parishioners can develop it with input from the Discovery Phase. Further planning is most effective when driven by a mission statement, a commonly accepted articulation of identity and purpose. Its translation into daily life can be enhanced by an accompanying expression of core values. These values can then serve as topics for further exploration in the Design Phase. Figure 3, below, is an example of a mission statement with core values from a parish.

Figure 3

Mission Statement and Core Values

We are the people of St. _____ Catholic Church, a spirited community of faith dedicated to **Welcome**, **Celebrate**, **Care**, and **Grow** in the image and likeness of Jesus.

We welcome by...
- Warmly receiving each person
- Inviting all to participate
- Affirming the goodness of all people

We care by...
- Respecting all life
- Sharing in times of joy and sorrow
- Showing love and compassion for others
- aiding those in need in our community and beyond

We celebrate by...
- Participating in the liturgy and sacraments
- Coming together in prayer
- Gathering in friendship

We grow by...
- Participating in quality Catholic education programs
- Experiencing spiritual development opportunities
- Sharing our gifts with others
- Nurturing our personal spirituality

---

3. Design Phase

The Design Phase uses input from the previous phases to surface concrete ways of enhancing parish life. "How to do it?" is the guiding question in this phase. As an example, we will use the parish whose mission statement and core values we cited in Figure 3. After developing their mission statement and list of core values, parish leaders planned a town hall meeting to identify specific ways to implement the core values of their mission statement. The first core value, "welcome," was described in a brief statement that serves as a kind of "provocative proposition":

> As a parish, we value being a warm and welcoming community. We want to welcome all people—different people with different gifts—to fully participate in our worship, teaching, service and ministry.

Participants were then asked to share their responses to the following two appreciative questions about "welcome":

- Describe a time when you felt we truly conveyed an inviting and welcoming community to people. What do we do best to welcome people?
- As you look to the future, can you imagine one thing we might do that would really encourage more people to feel welcome and to participate in parish life?

The first question further explores the word "welcome." It asks when and where it has been at its best in the parish, and what makes it possible. The second question envisions possibilities for enhancing or maximizing the potential of "welcome." Notice how the first question centers participants in their best experience of welcoming, while the second asks ways to enhance welcoming. With their "best moments" actively in mind, parishioners are mentally in position to envision a desired future. This same process was carried out for each of the core values in their mission statement.

From the recommendations of town hall participants, the parish's planning committee developed goals and strategies for implementing the core values. Action steps were then clarified, prioritized, and formed into an action plan with assigned responsibilities, benchmarks for evaluating progress, and a timeline. In this way leaders created an entire strategic plan for their parish, one that was mission-centered and ready for implementation.

4. Destiny Phase

The Destiny Phase is the implementation of Appreciative Inquiry. This is the "Do it" phase, where the parish enacts the plan in concrete actions. Integral to the effective implementation of the plan is the creation of a more appreciative parish culture and an emphasis upon continuous learning, reassessment, and innovation. Are the actions undertaken effectively bringing the parish's mission and core values to life? This sort of evaluation should be carried out in a positive and appreciative manner, just as it was throughout the planning process. Appreciative Inquiry aims at a discourse about seeing and celebrating life.

Conclusion

In this chapter, we defined Appreciative Inquiry and showed its spiritual underpinnings. Christian faith, we saw, is about life in abundance. It is about what St. Paul called the truth, honesty, justice, purity, love, grace, and excellence that people encounter in a Christian community. To be sure, parishes have problems, and a council has to address them. Appreciative Inquiry helps council members to recognize that understanding, appreciating, and enhancing parish life are the heart of the matter, and in fact provide the most effective way to approach any problem. It is also based on well-tested organizational principles and experiences.

We must always remember that central to the church's mission is being the herald of the Good News. Appreciative Inquiry creates a culture of "good news" by making the parish a place where people tell stories about God in their lives, and where people implement life-giving actions. Are people in your parish excited because they are talking about the things they most deeply value? Are they discussing and implementing those things that give life? Do they see the good that the parish does, and do they make increasing that good the focus of discussion? If not, a change of culture is needed. That change can begin by engaging the power of Appreciative Inquiry.

CHAPTER SIX

Demographic Information as an Aid to Parish Planning

George Cobb

One of my first official visits as director of planning for the Diocese of Charlotte was with the pastoral council of a fairly affluent parish. To acquaint me with the parish they described the parish structure, naming all of the various commissions and committees. This list of commissions and committees did not include an organization concerned with social justice. When I asked them about the omission they explained that they did not have any "poor people" in the parish. Why should they divert parish resources, they asked, to establish a ministry that would have so little to do?

Their comments took me aback. However, I had with me a statistical profile of the parish, prepared by my office. It contained basic demographic information about the parish, including median income for neighborhoods within the parish. This information amazed the councillors.

They had not known that many neighborhoods were areas of low median income. They quickly concluded that the economic needs in the parish were greater than they had thought. Within a few months, parishioners established a social justice commission to work with other churches in the area to provide both a food pantry and a secondhand clothing outlet.

My encounter with this parish taught me two things. First, that some Catholics have a far too narrow understanding of parish. They think the parish consists only of active parishioners, people who attend Mass on Sunday. Second, that demographic information can be a valuable resource in planning parish ministries.

Parishes with modern computers have access to tremendous amounts of demographic information that can assist in planning. With this information, church officials at all levels can better understand the parish reality and its impact on ministries and parishioners. This chapter will outline the reasons why councils need statistical information. It will also show how this information can be useful in ministry. It will consider what information is most useful in planning. And it will discuss low-cost sources of statistical information about the parish, and how to present it in the most useful way.

The Vocation of Pastoral Councils

Consulting the *Code of Canon Law*[1] helps to develop a sense of the vocation of parish pastoral councils. Several canons deal with the definition of a parish, the scope of the pastor's responsibilities, and the role of the parish council in addressing these responsibilities.

Canon 515 states that the parish is "a certain community of the Christian faithful stably constituted in a particular church." As a general rule a parish is territorial. It embraces *all* the Christian faithful who live within certain geographic boundaries. But our understanding of the gospel message calls us to embrace everyone within that territory, Christian or not.

According to canon 536, the role of the parish pastoral council is to "give their assistance in fostering pastoral activity." In other words, their role is an extension of the pastor's responsibility to care for the community. The fundamental duties of a pastor are defined in canons 528-530. Canon 528.1

states that the pastor "is obliged to make provision so that the word of God is proclaimed in its entirety to those living in the parish." I believe that these phrases—"its entirety" and "living in the parish"—are central to this norm's interpretation. There are many faithful people living in Catholic parishes who are unknown to the pastor. Demographic information can help him recognize all those for whom he shares responsibility.

Canon 528.2 states that a pastor "is to see to it that the Most Holy Eucharist is the center of the parish assembly of the faithful. He is to work so that the Christian faithful are nourished through the devout celebration of the sacraments." In other words, the pastor has to make the Eucharist central to the life of all the parish's people, and to foster their participation.

"In order to fulfill his office diligently," explains canon 529.1, "the pastor is to know the faithful entrusted to his care." This canon emphasizes the need for information about the wider community within the parish. To know his people, a pastor must seek them out and discover their needs. Some faithful people are not able to attend Mass. They are not to be neglected.

If the parish is all the people living within certain geographic boundaries, the parish council cannot simply look at those people who attend weekend Mass. It has to look further. If the council is to reflect on the diversity of the people of the parish, information about the socioeconomic make-up of the people is required. Good socioeconomic information insures that the ministries of the faith community meet the needs of those they are called to serve. If the pastoral council is to effectively assist the pastor in fostering pastoral activity, accurate demographic information is necessary. Without accurate information the council's knowledge of the parish is limited. Accurate information, presented in both text and graphics, informs the council, reinforcing—and at times correcting—anecdotal impressions.

The Uses of Demographic Information

The following two stories illustrate how demographic information can be used in a pastoral setting. The first story concerns a small parish in the western part of North Carolina. This parish is in the Appalachia area. The pastoral council knew that the median income in the parish was below the median income for the state. Knowing this, however, was of little help to ministry planners. They recognized that the needs of poor parishioners were enormous, so overwhelming that the parish felt paralyzed. They did not know where to start.

The pastor and council needed more specific information, and they needed it in a form that was easy for parishioners to understand. When they decided to revise their pastoral plan they asked the diocesan planning office for help. The office created a series of maps of the parish based on information from the 1990 U.S. Census and other data that updated the Census information. The maps divided the parish into neighborhood areas ("block groups" in census terms). The maps distinguished impoverished areas from those with higher income. Quantifying data was presented in addition to the maps. This data gave the median income for each neighborhood, the size of households, and the ethnicity of the residents. Together, the maps and tables drew a picture of the poverty in the parish, clarifying areas of need and heightening awareness. The council shared the information with ministry heads in the parish, enabling them to define the actions that would reach out to the neediest people.

The second story is about discussions the Diocese of Charlotte facilitated a couple of years ago among parishes to determine the location of a new high school. Since the area could support only one high school, heated debates occurred over its location. Various groups argued in favor of sites close to their own communities. To clarify the discussion, a series of maps was developed that showed growth, population density, and Catholic population. The maps were over-laid, giving a "three-dimensional look" at the area. The maps provided a strong visual image of the relevant demographic information. In addition, the maps showed highway access to the proposed sites so that could be easily evaluated. This information helped the committee achieve a consensus on the best location. Later, the maps proved useful in fund-raising since they documented not only the current need but also the anticipated growth the site was selected to meet.

Since 1990, the Catholic population of the Diocese of Charlotte has grown about 7.5% per year. In some areas growth is as much as 18%. This much growth exerts tremendous pressure for the development of new parishes and schools. Trying to locate where these new parishes and schools should go is a major concern at both the parish and diocesan level. Data collected and mapped allow diocesan officials to monitor growth on a consistent basis. The ability to accurately monitor growth has greatly improved the accuracy of recommendations for future parishes and schools. Having this data available in an easily understood format has speeded recommendations and saved thousands of dollars in consulting fees.

As illustrated in the school story, population growth information is extremely helpful in determining the location of a parish or school. The Diocese of Charlotte is still very rural—often one church serves a whole county. As development occurs, pressure builds on pastoral councils to move the parish church and other buildings from the downtown of a small city to a suburban location. Maps locating growth and parishioner households have been extremely helpful guides in purchasing land for future parishes or in deciding to move parish buildings if planning studies indicate a move is necessary.

Kinds of Demographic Information

Pastoral councils need good demographic information for planning. But not all information is equally useful. Information-gathering agencies publish far more data than any group of parishioners can possibly digest. Council members must discern what is useful and what is not. If they fail to make the distinction, they run into trouble, as the following story shows.

The Diocese of Charlotte has a set outline for parish re-evaluation that each parish is to follow before beginning a capital campaign. The outline lists the information that the parish needs in order to evaluate its ministries, estimate projected needs, and properly plan for the future. The pastor and pastoral council of a parish in the northern part of the diocese spent six months drafting a document based on this outline. They gathered a two-inch thick sheaf of demographic information from various sources in the parish. Often, the information from one source contradicted that from another. Parish leaders had made no effort to resolve the conflicts in the information or to use it to evaluate parish ministries. They simply collected data. They never stopped to reflect on what it meant for parish ministries or the proposed building. To estimate projected needs they surveyed parishioners and compiled the results.

Members of parish commissions were not given an opportunity to review data, set goals or objectives, or give input into the project to be constructed. When the council presented the data to the diocesan planning office they felt pressed to begin construction. But their plan was rejected, construction was delayed, and the faith community was frustrated. To avoid repeating this problem the diocesan planning office now supplies the information the council needs for planning so that the council can spend its time analyzing the data and developing ministry goals.

The typical profile package of information provided by the Diocese of Charlotte is specific to the territory of the parish. This package includes:[2]

- 1990 Population
- Current Year (CY) Population Estimates
- CY plus five Population Estimates
- 1990 Households
- CY Household Estimates
- CY plus 5 Household Estimates
- Household Change 1990 to CY
- 1990 and CY Median Household Income
- CY Employment
- CY Number of Households by Income
- CY Percentage by Race
- CY Ethnicity Estimates
- CY Percentage by Gender
- CY Population by Age
- 1990 and CY Median Age
- Area (Square Miles)

These sixteen fields of information compose the data that parishes find most useful. With this information councils can define how many people reside in the parish's census area, the median age of the population, the number of family households, including one-parent families, and a host of other matters. Wisdom dictates that the package cannot contain more that the average person can absorb. Additional information can be provided if a need arises.

The Diocese of Charlotte has learned that a good starting point in discussing ministries in a parish is a descriptive map. The diocese generates professional quality maps using computer-based mapping. These maps are designed to show the level of detail that will be most useful for parish planning. They are greatly appreciated at the parish level.

For example, figures 1 and 2 show median income in the Appalachia area of Western North Carolina. The locations of Catholic churches are identified with a circle. St. John the Evangelist Parish is located in Haywood County, indicated by the white lines on the map. Figure 1 shows the median income of Haywood County and neighboring counties by census tract.

Median income is an important variable to be considered in planning because median income determines poverty. Areas of poverty offer a host of ministry opportunities ranging from homeless shelters to educa-

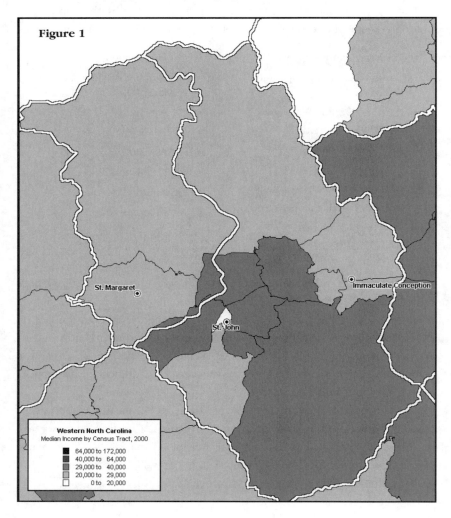

Figure 1

Western North Carolina
Median Income by Census Tract, 2000

■ 64,000 to 172,000
■ 40,000 to 64,000
■ 29,000 to 40,000
□ 20,000 to 29,000
□   0 to 20,000

tion programs. A map showing the median income of an entire county may not be detailed enough to indicate locations of poverty. Census tract maps offer greater detail but still may not be detailed enough to identify low-income areas in some parishes. In these cases block group data is required to aid the parish in identifying areas of need.

On the census tract map shown in figure 1, St. John the Evangelist church is located in an area of poverty surrounded by large areas of affluence. However, figure 2, a map based on block groups, clearly dis-

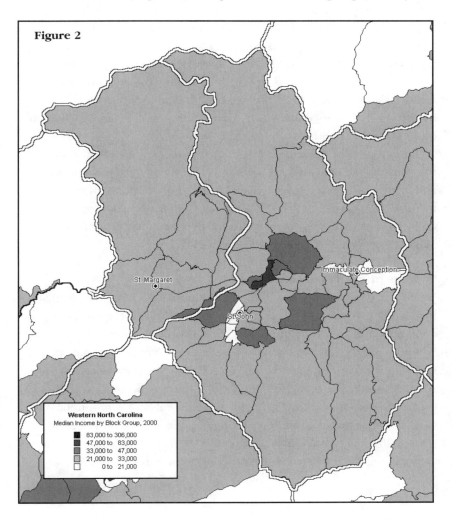

Figure 2

Western North Carolina
Median Income by Block Group, 2000

83,000 to 306,000
47,000 to 83,000
33,000 to 47,000
21,000 to 33,000
0 to 21,000

tinguishes higher income areas from lower income areas. Since these maps are linked to numerical data, tables can be generated to show median income by census tracts or block groups based on the planning needs of the parish.

Another map included in the resources supplied by the Diocese of Charlotte assists parish planners to see where parishioners live. This map is generated by entering into the system the numbers of Catholic households in each zip code. This map usually piques council members' interest and sparks a great deal of discussion. Understanding where parishioners live has ramifications for program development. For instance, some of the mountain parishes of the Diocese of Charlotte have difficulty building a sense of parish life because of the distances from church. On a map distances may seem small, but driving the winding mountain roads is slow, especially if the weather is bad. Knowing this has led these parishes to establish small communities of faith and to schedule more activities on Sunday.

A demographic package consisting of numerical data to complement the maps is also designed for the parish. This package shows population and economic trends, ethnicity, gender make-up, population by age, and income comparison figures. The final element of the package are tables outlining parish trends in reception of the sacraments, faith formation, Mass attendance, and registered households.

Sources of Information

When the diocese does not serve as the primary source of information for planning, the parish can do this for itself. All that is required is a good computer and a little money. The first problem encountered will be where to get the data. Since most parishes have neither the staff to gather information nor unlimited budget to obtain data, they will need to find sources to provide accurate demographic information. Fortunately, this problem is easily solved. Countless government and semi-public agencies gather this information on an ongoing basis. Often it is free for the asking, and much of it is available on the internet. The three best sources of demographic information are described in the next paragraphs.

The United States Census Bureau

The largest source of information is the U.S. Census Bureau. It is the only complete, 100% count of the general population. It presents demographic details down to the city block. The Census is invaluable for planning ministries within the parish boundaries. Buying data directly from the Census can be prohibitive, but much Census information can be borrowed from a library. Most local libraries have at least the information for their own area. University libraries are frequently federal depositories of information where the complete Census is available on CD-ROM.

In addition to the general census that occurs every ten years, the Census Bureau updates information on particular aspects of the population by conducting special censuses. These are supplemented by special studies done by other federal agencies, most notably the Bureau of Economic Analysis, the U.S. Dept of Health and Human Services, and the U.S. Department of Labor. All of these agencies collect information on the latest national trends, usually updating them every two years. Additional estimates and projections take place on the regional and state level.

Local and State Sources

The U.S. Census Bureau also works with local governments to produce two major studies. The first is a neighborhood analysis based on the general census for special areas within a community. The Census Bureau and the U.S. Department of Housing and Urban Development publish these neighborhood analyses. They identify low-income areas of a city. Not all cities participate in these studies, but they are definitely a valuable source of information where they are available.

A second cooperative study is done under the auspices of the U.S. Department of Transportation by Metropolitan Planning Organizations (MPOs). MPOs are local political bodies responsible for transportation planning across the nation. An MPO is established in every community of 50,000 persons or more. They collect data similar to that of the census, but the areas studied are smaller than the census tract level. The MPOs update data at least once between censuses. As public information these data are available to anyone at little or no cost.

The state data center is probably the largest depository of information for both the federal and state level. All information produced by the Census Bureau for the state is kept at the state data center. In addition, the state also keeps data on the county level and makes estimates or projections for each county or city within the state's jurisdiction. Often, this is the only source for projections below the state level and, for local agencies, the only "official" projections they can publish. The state data center is usually located at the state library or at a central university. Their greatest strength is that data are updated on an annual basis. The data are also consistent across the entire state. Their biggest weakness is that the data are reported only on the county level, usually too gross a scale for parish analysis. But the data are still useful in indicating trends for a particular county or region of the state.

Other state agencies acquire and report data. Normally these data are specific to the agency's interests and are updated on an annual or biannual basis. As with the state data center this information is accumulated on the state and county level. This can be good information for analyzing trends by county.

Local and city governments also collect demographic information about their citizens. This information includes growth patterns and population estimates. Normally it is available at a small charge or even at no charge to non-profit organizations. Two problems are encountered with local data. First, it is often available only in larger cities. Second, it is not gathered consistently from year to year. Such local data may help a few communities within a large diocese, but not all. The rest of the diocese will depend on the U.S. Census or the state data center.

Private Sources

Private sources of demographic data, such as MapInfo and TargetPro, are usually more expensive than public sources. But they may be the only way to have consistent, complete data between censuses on the subcounty level across a large geographic area. Many companies offer various add-ons to their basic package that parish planners may find unnecessary. The wisest planners know what they need, buy only that, and shop around for the best prices.

In short, the U.S. Census is the most important and least expensive source of information for pastoral planners. It is detailed down to the city block. Its greatest limitation is that it takes place only every ten years and planners need to update information every three to five years. Federal, state, and local bodies do other studies that can supplement previous census figures. These studies are inexpensive and easily available through state data centers. The Diocese of Charlotte updates its U.S. Census data through TargetPro. This is more expensive than public sources but it enables the diocese to keep accurate statistics across the entire diocese.

Presentation of Data

I have been to meetings where researchers pull out reams of paper with table after table of numbers. The numbers describe demographic data and growth, well-researched and accurate, in mind-numbing detail. Non-researchers respond to these presentations with a few nods—or worse, with eyes-glazed-over stares. The data are not meaningful to them. If researchers present the same information with a color chart or map, laypeople will study it—if for no other reason than to find their parish and their house. Color charts and maps win people's attention.

One does not have to be a professional researcher to create charts and maps that will engage parishioners. With a good computer and adequate programs, a knowledgeable person can create excellent parish maps. Anyone with a good computer can access and use much of the data mentioned in the previous paragraphs. This information can be presented graphically to a pastoral council or a parish assembly. Creating basic presentations is not hard with the right software and hardware, even for a novice. Sophisticated presentations, however, require the expertise of a professional planner or demographer.

Hardware and Software

The age of computers has brought the advent of desktop computer mapping. Any planner with a Pentium computer or better has access to an unlimited amount of information that can be presented graphically. Initial graphic presentations may be created using tables or charts, but eventually, maps are the most desirable graphic presentation for specialized purposes.

All of the mapping and data needed for parish planning can be obtained through the Census Bureau and their TIGER (Topologically Integrated Geographic Encoding and Referencing System) files. These TIGER files are available at the same places as the Census data. A TIGER conversion program and mapping software must be purchased. Several are available on the market today, popular ones being ARCVIEW and MAPINFO. The Diocese of Charlotte uses MAPINFO from MapInfo Corporation[3] because of its long track record of stability, quick training, ease of use, and customer support. The TIGER conversion software we have used in the past is the Universal Tiger Translator (UTT) from International Computer Works International.[4] This program translates Census TIGER files into a format that can be read by MAPINFO. The work of converting TIGER files can be avoided by purchasing International Computer Works translation of the entire United States. The translator and MAPINFO packages together cost about $2,000, a small amount to pay for so much valuable information.

Another option for mapping demographics is the U.S. Census Bureau's TIGER Mapping Service (TMS). It is available at the U.S. Census web site: HTTP://tiger.census.gov. While this allows planners to present information in map form, it does not allow reconfiguration of data. This prevents adding data to the system or customizing the presentation.

Once data is acquired and maps are translated it is not difficult to set up a simple Geographic Information System (GIS). The Diocese of Charlotte set up our GIS with a Pentium 133 with 64 megabytes of RAM. This should be considered minimum for startup. The system was upgraded recently to a Pentium II with 256 megabytes of RAM. This has improved performance. Data and maps are disk-intensive so a large hard drive is essential, the bigger the better. A ten-gigabyte hard drive should be considered minimum. Printing is now done on a Hewlett Packard (HP) 2250TN with 80 megabytes of RAM but good maps can be produced on a HP890.

A large plotter that permits printing 24" X 36" maps or greater is helpful. Nothing is better for presentations than to be able to print out large maps that can be clearly seen. In addition, for group workshops these larger maps are helpful in allowing people to draw and mark up their ideas. A Hewlett Packard 750C has been used at the diocese for four years with no difficulties. This has allowed us the flexibility to do just about any size map needed.

In summary, modern computers allow pastoral planners to access a mountain of demographic data. This data can overwhelm parishioners. For that reason, I recommend that planners be selective about what they present. Furthermore, I advise the use of color maps and charts to make demographic data understandable. Parish planners without the support of a diocesan planning office can access maps and data from the U.S. Census Bureau using its on-line TIGER mapping. Professional planners can create a more sophisticated GIS. This has the capability of adding data to that supplied by the Census Bureau. It can also reconfigure Census data. By presenting demographic data in a graphic format, pastoral planners can really grab the attention of parishioners.

Conclusion

Parish pastoral councils have the task of helping to foster pastoral activity within the parish. The parish consists of more than the active parishioners; it includes all the Christian faithful within the parish's territory. When the council fosters pastoral activity, it shares in the ministry of the pastor, announcing the Good News to all the people living in the parish. If the council is properly to assist in fostering pastoral activity, it must help the pastor know the parish and the people living in it.

Accurate demographic information is essential for knowing the parish. Without such information, people know the parish via personal impressions and anecdotes. Demographic information complements subjective knowledge and sometimes corrects it. Such information can help the parish plan for ministry by clarifying the parish's needs. It can also help planners lay the necessary groundwork for capital improvements at the parish and diocesan level.

This chapter described the kinds of information that are most useful to parish planners. The sixteen basic fields of census data offer planners invaluable information about the parish population, income, and households. This basic data can move pastoral councils from sweeping generalizations about the parish to more accurate perceptions. It can enable the council to plan for ministries that meet the real needs of the people.

Demographic information supplied by the U.S. Census is inexpensive and easily accessible. The Census Bureau itself, as well as federal, state, and local bodies, tracks developments during the period between the national censuses. Private companies compile this information and, for a fee, make it available to planners. Parishes with the basic census data, updated information, and projections can describe themselves and anticipate future developments.

Basic demographic information is available to individual parishes with good computers, adequate software, and knowledgeable parishioners with an interest in demographics. By showing parish maps that indicate the findings of the national Census, pastoral councillors can awaken interest in the true state of the parish. They can create customized maps that show the relevance of census data to a parish's ministry and future. If councils are to aid the pastor in knowing the parish and planning for it, demographic information is indispensable. Councils should insist on it.

PART IV

Planning for the Future

CHAPTER SEVEN

Planning:
Idol or Icon
of Pastoral Councils?

John Flaherty

At root, the words "idol" and "icon"[1] mean the same thing. Both words refer to an image. Yet, for Christians, the terms have radically different connotations. An icon is an imperfect window that gives insight into a reality beyond itself. Traditionally, an icon is an image of a thing that is holy. By means of intuition and imagination, the icon points beyond itself and gives insight into a holy reality. The reality is more important than the image, yet the image is an indispensable tool in gaining access to the reality to which it points. An idol, on the other hand, is a thing elevated to the status of divinity. It does not point to something else. It is an end in itself.

Pastoral planning is like an icon. It invites all those involved to contemplate the ministry of the parish as a whole and to see in it the pastoral ministry of the universal church. It draws everyone more deeply into the ultimate purpose, or mission, of the church. Planning is not an idol. It is not an end in itself. It is rather an icon of the church's mission. I believe that such planning is the essential ministry—indeed the indispensable tool—of a parish pastoral council.

Parishes cannot simply gauge their success by how many people attend an event at the parish center, or how much money they raise, or how many programs they have, or how nice their buildings are. Instead, parishes need to measure success by how well people bring the word of God into their homes, neighborhoods, and workplaces. The critical questions are: "Are people giving witness by living holy lives? Are they transforming the world by their influence on economics and politics? Is the word of God being made known?" Parish effectiveness ought to be measured by the extent to which parishioners are enabled to fulfill the greater mission of the church. The parish pastoral council, in my view, should help make these connections.

A key word to consider when reflecting on the role of a pastoral council is precisely the word "pastoral." What does it mean to be pastoral? It is hard to find a common definition. To some people, pastoral simply means "being nice." The pastoral thing to do is the nice thing to do. From this viewpoint, pastoral is a style of relating. When people say, "We want a pastoral priest," they often mean, "we want a nice guy." Pastoral, however, means more than being nice.

George Wilson, S.J., has written a thought-provoking article on what it means to be pastoral.[2] "Pastoral" does not have to do with the kind of person one is or the kind of job one has, he writes, but how one applies the teachings of the church. Sometimes that means anything but being nice. It involves "tough love," that is, saying difficult things that need to be said. Being pastoral includes saying challenging, prophetic words about issues that need to be addressed.

Pastoral, in its broadest sense, refers to the "self-realizing activity of the church"; that is, taking what the church teaches and applying it to concrete, changing circumstances. Everyone wants to be pastoral. But it is an extremely difficult, challenging task that needs to be approached with a certain amount of humility.

How does the parish pastoral council relate to this "self-realizing activity of the church"? In my view, the council draws all other parish ministries into the big picture—a vision of the whole. The council looks at the parish and asks, "How do all of these programs and activities relate to the mission of the church? How are we, as a parish, changing the world? How can we more effectively cooperate with the Holy Spirit to manifest and extend the kingdom of God?"

The most effective way for the parish pastoral council to exercise its function, I believe, is through long-range planning. Long-range planning assesses current realities, develops a vision for the future, sets goals directed at accomplishing that vision, and strategizes about the tasks or activities that will achieve the goals. This sort of planning is an essential activity of the council even when it is not the only activity. Other council activities (e.g., coordinating parish events and ministry efforts, dealing with crises, taking complaints, etc.) should be derived from, or subsumed under, planning.

This chapter will show how planning can be an icon for parish pastoral councils. Icons are an aid to prayer, and so I will begin with a comparison of the liturgy to the pastoral council. Second, I will look at the roles of the pastoral council and the pastor. Next, my focus will be the nature of pastoral planning as a response to change in the parish. After that, I will look at the characteristics of the planning council. And finally, I will confront some obstacles to planning and suggest how to overcome them. The goal is to show that planning is not an idol or end in itself. It is rather an icon that helps pastoral councils see the reality of the church.

Liturgy as a Model

Liturgy and pastoral council activity are similar in some illuminating ways. Like council ministry, liturgy is an icon that connects us to deeper realities. Four liturgical principles reflect the true nature of parish planning. They are the principles of active participation, of various ministries, of church order, and of clarity of roles. A comparison between the liturgy and the pastoral council helps to illustrate why planning is fundamental to pastoral councils.

The first principle is that liturgy is **activity.** The Greek word, "liturgy" means the "work of the people." Planning is also the work of the people. The council represents that portion of the Body of Christ that is established as a parish. The council plans in the name of and on behalf of parishioners. It calls the people to work together just as they work together in liturgy. Sometimes the council explicitly calls the people together as part of the planning process. Most often the council acts on behalf of the whole as it plans.

A second principle is that a **variety of ministries** exists within liturgy. Similarly, within the parish, the charisms of God's people are brought forward for the good of the whole community in a variety of ways. One concern of pastoral councils is to recognize and coordinate this variety of ministries. In liturgy, the "ministry of the assembly" holds a central role. Parish councils, through planning, focus on the "ministry of the whole" to accomplish the ultimate parish purpose, carrying out the mission of the Christ.

A parish pastoral council needs to be aware that it is not planning for "those people," other parishioners, as if there were a radical separation between them and the council. Collaborating with the pastor, the council enables, empowers, and encourages all parishioners to undertake the mission of the church. The people of the parish are the active subjects, not the objects, of the council's ministry.

Another liturgical principle is that all **ministries are ordered** toward building up the Body of Christ in the community. The motive for planning is just this ordering of ministry. Planning helps the parish focus on accomplishing its mission. It mobilizes the resources and energies of the people toward this end. It also affirms and celebrates parish accomplishments. Whatever the plan looks like and however deep the parish commitment is to it, all must be ordered toward empowering the community as the visible Body of Christ.

In liturgical celebrations, each person is instructed to do all, but only, what pertains to his or her **role in liturgy**. The fourth principle holds true for pastoral councils. A variety of roles exists within the parish community. The most important is the role of all baptized Christians to evangelize the world and transform the temporal order. Distinct roles exist within that general call of all the baptized. Every ministry, lay as well as ordained, has expectations—that is, rights and obligations. In order to exercise their ministry appropriately, pastoral council members must become well versed in the expectations the church has for their ministry.

The Roles of Pastor and Council

The principles of liturgy illuminate the pastoral council as a planning body. As was just stated, in the liturgy, participants do only what pertains to their role. Let us look briefly at the roles of the pastor and of the pastoral council.

Just as the priest presides at liturgy, overseeing all of the ministries and drawing them into one complete act of worship, so does the pastor preside over the functioning of the council. The pastor is the leader and chief shepherd of the parish. He has many shepherding functions: organizing, planning, staffing, budgeting, reporting, coordinating, etc. The pastor is the head of the parish but the head does not function in isolation from the body. One link, often mandated by the local bishop, between the pastor, as the head, and the body, the parish, is the pastoral council. The council represents, that is, makes present, the Body of Christ, in the process of planning for the future of the community.

Two Latin words: "*consilium*" and "*concilium*" are translated into English as "council."[3] A *concilium* with a "c" is a legislative body that can issue dogmatic statements, decrees, and constitutions. The Second Vatican Council was a *concilium*. A *consilium* with an "s" is an advisory or consultative body. A parish pastoral council is a *consilium*. It cannot legislate. Much trouble arises when councils see themselves as legislative bodies with the pastor as the executive who has veto power over the legislation. In considering the roles of the pastor and the parish pastoral council, the first thing to keep firmly in mind is that the pastoral council is consultative, not legislative in nature.

Sometimes the words "consultative" and "advisory" are used interchangeably but I see a subtle, yet important, distinction between them. Consultation is a passive stance. It waits to be asked, "What do you think about this?" and "Should I do this or should I do that?" It means being engaged only when stimulated with a question. Advisory, on the other hand, assumes an active role. An advisor is always involved in deliberations by investigating, studying, researching, and praying about a situation. Advisors say, "We know that there is a trend in the parish and we think we need to address it." Councils, I believe, are not exclusively consultative or advisory in this sense of those terms. They are both.

In some circumstances the pastor will consult. For example, he may say to the council, "I have been listening to people in marriage instruction and in the confessional and I really think we need a renewal program. Before I plan too far ahead, I want to hear your opinions." He initiates the discussion. On the other hand, the pastoral council may advise him. It may say to the pastor, "We need to do things differently. We need to re-evangelize the converted. Maybe we need to look at a variety of opportunities for helping people get better in touch with their faith." In this case, the council takes the initiative. Both of these modes of operation are permissible.

Some envision a parish pastoral council that acts only when the pastor prompts it. These councils "sleep until the pastor rouses them." Such pastors solicit the advice of their councils and then "do their own thing." This is probably not the best use of a council. It lacks a full understanding of the nature of the council. A council that is actively involved in planning, particularly in the early stages of research as it listens to the parish and discerns God's Spirit at work among the people, makes more effective use of the gifts and talents of its members.

One way to clarify the meaning of the word "council" is to consider what a council is not. A council is not a *concilium,* a legislative body. A council is also not a grievance board. A council is not an administrative body, seeing to the day-to-day operations of the parish.[4] Councils go wrong when they try to be legislative bodies, boards of governors, or grievance boards. They can also be too involved with day-to-day administration. The parish pastoral council is not the finance council. In my view, the finance council should develop the budget as a resource plan that reflects and supports the long-range pastoral plan proposed by the pastoral council.

In short, pastors and councils have distinctive roles. The pastor presides. The council serves as a "consilium" but not a "concilium." The council may freely advise the pastor, and he freely consults the council. But the council does not legislate. Its ministry is pastoral planning, the topic to which we now turn.

Planning as Council Ministry
Planning always involves change. Change is inevitable. It will happen

whether or not it is planned. I believe that councils should direct change in the parish, rather than merely react to it. They have to recognize how significant change is. They need to acknowledge how awkward and painful it can be. And they should make sure that the conditions necessary for change are present before moving ahead. This is as true for the parish as a whole as it is for the council. (See Chapter Four "Involving the Whole Community" for a further discussion of the stages of change in an organization.)

The fundamental ministry of councils is pastoral planning. As councils take on a planning role, they should consider, assess, and, if necessary, act on these things:

- the nature of the proposed change;
- the situation that is being changed; and
- the task-relevant maturity of the participants.

Each of these three is an important part of the council's ministry. Each will be treated at some length below.

The Nature of Change

Councils have first to consider the nature, complexity, and difficulty of proposed change. Paul Dietterich, director of the Center for Parish Development in Chicago,[5] offers an analysis of the kinds of change parishes deal with. He says parishes face four kinds of change: **tuning, adapting, re-orienting,** and **re-creating.** He distinguishes among these types of change from two perspectives. On one hand, some change is incremental (such as tuning and adapting), other change is systemic (re-orienting and re-creating). Further, change can be reactive (adapting and re-creating). By "reactive," Dietterich means change that responds to external events. In this type of change, the church is *reacting* to a new environment or a new set of circumstances. By way of contrast, tuning and re-orienting are *anticipatory.* In these cases, change is initiated by the church *in anticipation* of external events. On the basis of this analysis, Dietterich observes, "The greater the degree of shock to the system (intensity) and the larger the number of interrelated organizational factors to be addressed (complexity), the more difficult the change process."[6]

This analysis of the types of change and their relative difficulty can be helpful as a parish approaches a possible change in the way the council operates. If a council wants to put greater emphasis on pastoral planning than it previously did, it must ask itself, "What is the nature of the change?" Does such a council need only to shift from coordinating parish activities to pastoral planning? Or does it need to reorient its basic relationship to parish life? Does this council think it is responsible for making the pastor accountable to the people? Or does this council think its purpose is to make sure that the parish is managed on a businesslike basis? If the council wants to put a greater emphasis on pastoral planning, it may require substantial reorientation, a much more complex task than merely tuning or adapting the council's efforts.

The Situation Being Changed

The next area to consider in directing change is the situation. In a parish, everything depends on the situation within which change actually takes place. The situation is the context for change. If councils want deliberate change to happen, then they must be sure that three conditions are present:

1. sufficient external pressure;

2. strong internal dissatisfaction (the *status quo* isn't working anymore); and

3. a compelling alternative vision.[7]

Consider the example of the council that wants to change itself. It wants to become more of a planning body. It wants to refocus its attention on long-range planning for the parish. How are these three conditions for change to be present in such a council? I will examine each of these three in turn.

1. External Pressure. The universal church itself exerts external pressure on parish pastoral councils to become planning bodies. Since Vatican II, the church has described itself in new ways. In changing the way it talks about itself, the church has not changed its essential nature. Rather, the church is trying to incorporate more of the truth into its language of self-expression. Let me give five examples of the way in which the church expresses itself differently since Vatican II. Each of them, it can be said, exerts pressure on the pastoral council to become more of a planning body.

First, consider the church's universality. Before Vatican II, when people in the church spoke of it as universal, they seemed to suggest that the church was a great monolith. It was the same everywhere. That changed when Vatican II described the universal church as a communion of local churches. Local communities have particular cultural, social, political, and economic experiences in which to carry out the gospel. This is an issue for planning. The question for the local community has become: "How can we be the best expression of church in this place at this time?"

A second instance has to do with shared responsibility. Many may have once thought of the church as only a "chain of command." In this chain, the pope gives orders to the bishops who then order the priests who then order the laity. Since Vatican II the church has included a more collegial vision of basic Christian equality rooted in baptism. If all share the church's mission to carry the gospel to the whole earth, then all should be fully, consciously, and actively involved in how to carry out that mission. In a collegial church, planning is not just a job for the hierarchy. It belongs as well to those at the local and parish level.

A renewed emphasis on the humanity of Jesus is a third instance of increasing pressure for pastoral planning. Catholics today continue to view Jesus as the incarnation of God's unchanging Word, but they also have a deeper insight into his human life. This impacts the way a parish sees its ministry. The Christian mission is not just to imitate timeless truths. That requires no deliberation. The mission also involves decisions about what it means to be a Christian of a particular race or ethnicity in a particular time and geographic location. It requires making the best choices for a specific situation.

A fourth instance of Vatican II change that applies pressure on the pastoral council has to do with the laity. The laity's sense of what is appropriate in faith has changed. People today are much less likely to accept church authority without question. Catholics today ask more questions. They also believe that the church is not a thing but a relationship between a person and the traditions of the community of faith. This leads to an expectation that Catholics will take a more active role in making decisions about how their faith is lived both as individuals and in the parish community.

A new understanding of community is a final instance of post-Vatican II pressure on councils to become planning bodies. Catholics no longer see religion as private and personal. They recognize its necessary communal aspect. Liturgy shows this most dramatically. Before Vatican II, people came back from communion and had a private moment with Jesus. Today many people pick up a hymnbook and sing. The church recognizes that each person's relationship with Jesus is created, formed, and nourished in the context of the community. This insight emphasizes shared values and common commitment. The communal aspect of faith is exercised by the parish pastoral council when it recommends the activities that will be undertaken in the name of the parish. The deliberation, discussion, and decisions required to move the parish forward in its common mission are all aspects of planning.

In summary, councils are to help direct change in a parish, not just to react passively. If they desire change in the parish, they must know whether the conditions for change are present. Without these conditions, change will be ineffective. One of these conditions is external pressure. There must be a strong force moving the parish. The developments in the church since Vatican II are an example of such a force. These developments apply force to parish pastoral councils. The teaching about the church as a local community, sharing responsibility in the name of the human Jesus, responding thoughtfully and with a consciousness of the church's communal dimension, are powerful developments. They provide a motive for councils to assume a pastoral planning role. Still, a second necessary condition for change is required, the condition of internal dissatisfaction.

2. **Internal Dissatisfaction**. The second condition for change, internal dissatisfaction, is more dependent on conditions in each parish. Certainly, a council that is effectively working with the pastor would have little motivation for change. That is not the situation that exists in

all parishes, though. In some parishes, pastors are not quite sure what to do with a council, but are willing in principle to work with one. In other places, council members themselves are dissatisfied with their role. To them, council ministry may seem to consist of nothing more than long, boring meetings with few concrete results. These councils would most likely be amenable to changing and adopting a planning role.

3. **Alternative Vision**. The third condition for change is the presence of a compelling alternative vision. Such a vision depends on the council's re-thinking its role, learning how to connect its purpose with the mission of the church, and re-educating itself with the church's teachings and information on planning methods. The compelling alternative vision for a parish contemplating a change in its pastoral council may come from undertaking an Appreciative Inquiry process, such as the one described by David DeLambo and Richard Krivanka in Chapter Five of this book. Such a process can stir revitalization, a renewed sense of worth, and incredible energy. The parish pastoral council has a critical role as the parish's primary change agent, directing it toward its ultimate mission.

The Task-Relevant Maturity of the Participants

In this examination of the council's planning ministry, two aspects of change have been examined. One is the nature of change itself. The church has a strong commitment to adapting and reorienting itself. A second aspect of change encompasses the conditions for change. If a change is to be effective, the three conditions of pressure, dissatisfaction, and vision must be present.

A third and final aspect of change has to do with maturity. As a pastoral council moves into a planning role, it needs to consider the task-relevant maturity of the participants. In other words, how much direction and support does the council need? I am not talking about the members' psychological maturity or their spiritual maturity. I am talking about the maturity relevant to the specific tasks of moving a parish into an explicitly mission-oriented plan.

Here is a story to illustrate my point. A young priest recently went into a parish to replace a retiring pastor. The new pastor had really bought into a vision of collegiality. He planned to come to the parish and hand it over to the people and empower them for mission. He thought they would jump for joy in their new ownership of church. When he offered his vision to the people, they said, "Father, just tell us what you want us to do." He said, "No, no. It's your church." And they said again, "Just tell us what you want us to do."

The new pastor failed to understand the task-relevant maturity of the people. He did not ask, "How well do they understand my vision? What is their need for direction and their need for support in order implement it?" He did not recognize that people who are accustomed to being dependent do not become independent and self-directed just because the pastor wants them to! This young pastor needed to consider, assess, and act on their task-relevant maturity before asking them to take an active role in their mission.

The concept of task-relevant maturity has been studied at some length. It is commonly described as "situational leadership," because it teaches that the maturity of followers depends on their situation and can grow.[8] Leaders should not use exclusively one style of leadership, but should adopt different styles as the situation requires. Here are four images taken from the world of sports that describe how leaders meet the needs of followers for direction and support. The pastor and/or the council should assess the situation and apply a style of leadership appropriate to the situation.

The first style is that of the general manager. He sits at the front desk, makes decisions, and is not particularly concerned about whether or not people feel supported by him. He figures out the right things to do for the organization and then does them. This style is primarily directive. When people need clear direction about what they are to do, this is the best style. The young pastor might have done well to initially adopt this style with his parishioners. They were used to strong direction from the previous pastor. The new pastor needed to give them strong directions. He needed to describe clearly a task for them and where he hoped his vision of parish would take them.

The second style is that of the coach. He is the person who wants to get the task done but who also needs to support the players. Winning coaches are good teachers and excellent motivators. Their style is appropriate when a group has a strong need for direction and a strong need for support. It is obviously the most time-consuming style of leadership. The new pastor might also have considered this style of leadership as a way of moving his people toward a fuller ownership of their role as parishioners.

A third style is that of the cheerleader. If participants are self-starters or initiators, they may not need a lot of direction. They already have the skills to do the task but they need support, encouragement, or "pats on the back." This style is primarily supportive and not directive. I know of a suburban parish where many of the people are executives. They run companies and consulting firms. As council members, they do not need a lot of direction about planning. But they do need a lot of support and encouragement to trust their abilities and to feel that they can do it.

The fourth style of leadership is that of the spectator. The spectator sits on the sidelines and observes the team at work. It is ideal for people who do not need a lot of direction, people who know what they are doing. They also need little support or affirmation because they have confidence in their abilities. This style may work in some parishes. But in others it may be an abdication of leadership.

As a council moves toward pastoral planning, it would be wise to consider its own task-relevant maturity. What direction and support does it need for the undertaking? Likewise, as the pastoral council considers parish planning, it should assess the task-relevant maturity of the participants. Incorporating an appropriate level of both direction and support into the process will go far in assuring success.

Characteristics of a Planner

Planning is difficult. Getting a clear picture of the parish reality, engaging the unknown, considering possible courses of action, and outlining actions to be taken in the future are all abstract, complicated, and time-consuming tasks. Here, I will consider the characteristics that need to be exercised by a planning group and some of the conditions that exist in parish life. Councillors who plan, I believe, need to have six characteristics. They must be:

- inquisitive (willing to explore the unknown);

- conceptually uninhibited (not afraid of new or different concepts);

- constructively competitive (able to create new ideas out of disagreements);

- practical (able to identify what can realistically be accomplished);

- tenaciously tolerant (able to hang in there when things get tough);

- multi-disciplined (possessing many different kinds of skills).

It is unlikely that every member of the planning group will possess all of these characteristics. One member may be more conceptually uninhibited than the others while tenacity may be the gift of another. It is sufficient if all of the characteristics are present in the group as long as the one possessing the relevant characteristic exercises it at the appropriate time.

Parish planning is complicated by the real conditions of parish life. A recent study published in the *Review of Religious Research*[9] gives a profile of Protestant ministers and their typical work. Even though Roman Catholic clergy were not part of the study, the findings about Protestant clergy are consistent with what I know about priests. The study found that the typical work of pastors was:

- taxing, fast-paced, and unrelenting;

- marked by brevity, fragmentation, and variety; and

- reflective of the preference of pastors for action over reflection and verbal over written interactions.

These characteristics of a pastor's activity and preferences directly conflict, I believe, with the characteristics of a good planner. Clergy generally do not prefer to be reflective; they prefer action because constant action is the only way they can keep up. People make requests and demands on them that are unrelenting and fast-paced. Caught up in the day-to-day reality of parish life, many pastors find it hard to see the value of planning.

It is not impossible, however, for pastors and other busy people to adopt a planning mentality. In the *Seven Habits of Highly Effective People*, Stephen Covey offers a helpful time management tool. Covey analyzes the tasks, demands, and commitments of daily life, categorizing them as "important"

or "not important," "urgent" or "not urgent." Some things are both important and urgent, such as medical emergencies, pressing problems, and
deadline-driven projects. They are first priorities. After that comes a second
tier of priorities. These are things that are urgent but not important, such
as phones ringing, interruptions, and some meetings. Meeting these
demands is often pleasant and immediately rewarding. Most people would
rather be personally engaged in helping others than involved in the more
abstract work of planning. But caution is needed. Many urgent activities
that capture our time and energy are, Covey says, unimportant in the long
run. A week or even a day later, they are forgotten.

These relatively unimportant but urgent demands crowd out work
that is important but not urgent. They take time and energy from important matters that need, but do not demand, attention. Covey defines
important but not urgent work as those things that produce results—
those things that contribute to mission, values, and higher goals. The
lack of urgency means that these important matters can be put off for
another time until the delay becomes dangerous or counter-productive.

Important but not urgent activities include many "pastoral" things.
Preventing problems, building relationships, taking time for spiritual
growth, recognizing new opportunities and planning—all of these are
not urgent but very important pastorally. They are exactly the role of the
pastoral council. A pastor may himself possess few of the characteristics
of a good planner, but he is wise to gather around him people who do.

With the council, the pastor regularly takes time to consider the life
of the parish. He and the council ask how the parish is living the mission of the church. Together they inquire about the ways that parishioners relate to the church, to one another, and to their local community. Together, they ensure a connection between the mission of the
church and the parish's life and ministry. It is absolutely essential to the
life of a mission-centered parish that this be done and done well.

Obstacles to Planning

This chapter has argued that pastoral planning is an icon. It helps pastors and councils look beyond superficial matters and focus instead on
the reality of the church. The work of the council has been explained by

comparing it to the liturgy. In both liturgies and council meetings, every-one has a role to play. The council's work of pastoral planning is to help the parish direct change, not just to react passively. Although it is hard to make time for the important but not urgent work of reflection, pas-tors and councils can cultivate the characteristics of a good planner.

The church has acquired much wisdom about consultation in the past forty years. But difficulties still arise, especially when councils try to focus more intensively on planning. Usually one of four conditions is the cause. First, the pastor and/or the council members may not know what to do. Second, they may know what to do but they do not know how to do it. Third, they may not believe that planning is an important endeavor. And fourth, they may not believe that planning is important *for them* to do. These conditions can cripple planning. Before the problem can be reme-died, the cause must be identified. Which of the four obstacles is it?

Some of these obstacles can be conquered more easily than others. The first two, for example, are matters of simple ignorance. When coun-cils do not know what to do or how to do it, they need comprehensive information. They can read about the work of pastoral councils and planning models that have worked in other parishes.

Conditions three and four are more difficult to remedy. People who believe that planning is unimportant in general or personally irrelevant can bring a council to a standstill. Three arguments, however, may per-suade reluctant planners. First is the argument from **efficiency**. Daily experience may cause some people to resist planning. Its payoff is hard to see. Many would prefer muddling through. Muddling through, how-ever, is time-consuming. Taking the time and effort to plan is more effi-cient in the long run. This message is not an easy sell to parishes; it sometimes takes some serious convincing. However, as the saying goes, "Nothing succeeds like success." A pastor and council who have a suc-cessful planning process can convince others of its value. The personal testimony of other pastors carries a lot of weight with priests.

Other negative attitudes and motivations lurk behind reasons three and four. A false understanding of divine providence is one such atti-tude. People will say, "There is no use in planning. It's all in God's hands. He'll take care of us." This attitude hearkens back to a belief that we are merely puppets in some divine drama. Such a false understanding lets us off the hook too easily. People with this attitude may be convinced by a second argument, the argument for **stewardship**. Planning is good stewardship. To be sure, God acts first in the drama of salvation. But we must cooperate. We have to do the best we can to respond to God's care. We are stewards of the resources that God has given us. Planning simply cannot be shrugged off as having no value.

A final negative attitude is the desire for immediate gratification. People want quick results for their efforts. In ministry, this desire often manifests itself in helping a particular person with a particular problem. At the end of the day a minister can say, "I helped someone today." Planning does not offer such immediate gratification. It may seem businesslike and impersonal. It requires patience and long-suffering, which nobody enjoys. Against our desire for immediate gratification a third argument may be persuasive. It is the argument that planning is an **icon**. Planning leads us into a deeper perception of Christian reality. Planning calls people to look past what is right in front of them and look to the horizon. It is an icon that gives people a long-range view.

In order to make planning a primary activity of councils, these obstacles need to be addressed. The best arguments for planning are that it is efficient, that it manifests good stewardship, and that it is an icon leading to a deeper understanding. Commitment to a vision of the big picture and the ultimate meaning and purpose of all parish activities can provide the necessary motivation to plan.

Conclusion

To look deeply into the ministry of parish pastoral councils is to see the parish in relation to the universal church, to appreciate the connection of the parish to Catholics throughout the world, to recognize the bonds of Tradition that hold us together, and to act on the call to cooperate with the Holy Spirit in carrying out the commission of Christ. The parish pastoral council exercises its ministry most effectively by planning for the future. The act of planning is an icon, not an idol. It is not an end in itself, but the means by which the mission of the church is projected into the future.

Pastoral councils are under increasing pressure to take on a planning role. This pressure comes from two sources: 1) changes in the church's own self-understanding and self-expression and 2) dissatisfaction with parish councils expressed by pastors and council members. By focusing on the teachings of the church and its self-described role in the modern world and on the way the parish exercises that role, a pastoral council can become both a clear expression of the true church and an effective means of realizing its mission.

Pastoral councils anticipate, direct, and help manage change in the parish through a well-thought-out planning process. Working with the pastor (and other parish leaders, when necessary), they connect the parish to a vision of the greater church, assess the current situation, consider possible courses of action for the future, and develop goals and action plans. The action plans include means of reporting, evaluating, and celebrating success as well as reporting, evaluating, and adjusting when things do not go as planned.

The main obstacles to planning encountered by pastoral councils include uncertainty about their role and ignorance of planning processes as well as concern that the time and effort required by planning will be wasted. These obstacles can all be overcome. Most dioceses and archdioceses have published norms for parish pastoral councils that are available from the diocesan offices. In addition, many dioceses have a staff person who will come to the parish and help the council implement the norms. Most parishes have members who are familiar with planning through their workplaces. Schools, municipalities, hospitals, and government service are but a few of the training grounds for planning. Concern about wasting time and effort can be relieved by talking with parishes that have had a satisfactory experience with planning.

Planning is not an idol, a thing to be admired for itself. Planning is an icon, a window through which to see the reality of church and the parish experience of church. It is also an instrument for accomplishing our Christian mission. It is an essential role for the parish pastoral council.

CHAPTER EIGHT

How Do We Get There From Here?
A Planning Model

Mary Margaret Raley

Before a family can decide to go on a vacation trip, several big questions need to be answered:

- How much will it cost?
- Do we have the resources?
- Where will we go?
- How long will we be gone?

The answers to these questions depend on one another. For instance, how much the trip will cost depends on where the family wants to go and how long the members want to be away. How long they will be away depends on the availability of resources. Resources depend on where the family goes—and so on. Deciding to go on a family trip can be a fairly complicated decision-making process. But families do it all the time, usually without a whole lot of trouble or fanfare.

Strategic, or long-range, parish planning involves decision-making processes similar to those of a family anticipating a vacation trip. These aren't easy processes. They are not skills that people are born with. They involve getting unclear or contingent answers to critical questions. They might create frustrations because they can't create resources that don't exist. And planning alone doesn't assure a happy or successful outcome. The best-planned vacation can be ruined by nasty weather or lost luggage.

Nonetheless, planning skills are worth having, as the vacation-bound family is well aware. Even incomplete or poorly done planning is better than no planning. It can help people work together in happy and effective ways. It can increase the value of existing resources. And it can assure a better future together.

This chapter is a summary of a planning process. It will describe how planning actually happens, meeting by meeting, exercise by exercise, step by step. Other chapters in this book present readers with the theory of planning. They treat subjects such as involving the parish in organization development, Appreciative Inquiry, and the importance of demographic information. This chapter will focus, not on theory, but on practice. Presupposing the theories, it describes the tasks to be performed, the questions to be answered, and a few practical tools or techniques helpful in group planning.

After a few words about the planning team and their role in designing the process, each step in planning will be described. These steps will be enfleshed with associated exercises and instructions for their use.

The Planning Team

Pastors initiate consultation in order to involve the community and to draw upon the wisdom of the parishioners. Parish pastoral councils can be convoked only in the presence of a pastor. However, some parishes have no resident pastor; in others a pastoral life coordinator or pastoral administrator provides pastoral leadership for the parish community. In all these cases, pastoral leadership is well advised to seek parishioners' input. This planning model is not useful only for pastoral councils. It can be employed by all sorts of groups and organizations within a parish.

This chapter speaks of a "planning team" rather than the pastoral council. Usually, the pastoral council is the group charged with strategic planning. However, in some parishes planning is not done by the council itself but by a committee of the council. In other parishes the pastor may establish a separate group for the purposes of planning. The phrase "planning team" is meant to encompass all these possibilities.

The pastor or coordinator does not need to serve on every planning team but he or she certainly must be kept fully informed about the conversations and recommendations of the planning team. When the planning team is the parish pastoral council, the pastor is not a member; he is the presider. When planning centers on the activities of one group in the parish only those with a vital interest in that group serve on the planning team. For instance, a planning team for youth ministry would involve the youth minister, parents, youth, and others involved in that ministry. The pastor, pastoral life coordinator, or pastoral administrator should be actively involved in all general parish planning.

Members of a planning team might be members of the pastoral council or finance council, staff members interested in implementing the plan, parishioners in leadership positions, and others who may have valuable input into the planning process. Parishioners trained in planning for their career or work can be helpful in planning if they can put aside a desire for business-like efficiency and adopt an open stance toward the difficulties, complexities, and imperfections of pastoral planning.

A planning team designs the planning process, sets a timeline for its accomplishment, and schedules the meetings. Some planning can be accomplished in a single, daylong session. Other kinds of planning require a series of meetings. In general, these meetings are most efficient when they occur closely together. Each member of the planning team must be committed to the process and strive to participate in each meeting.

Once the planning team has been formed, everyone must become clear about the roles each will play in the process. When roles are clear, people feel empowered. In pastoral planning, some parishioners are action-takers or implementers. Some evaluate existing parish ministries, others recommend new ministries. The pastor is the final decision-maker. The exercise described by George Wilson in Chapter Four of this book, "Who Plays Which Roles?" develops clarity about the roles that will be played in the planning process, especially who will be deciding and implementing the plan. Clarity is crucial to the plan's success.

Next, the planning team reviews the tools for planning. In this chapter, the tools are grouped under three headings, "investigating," "considering," and "recommending." These correspond to the original threefold task of diocesan pastoral councils described by Vatican II documents. The tools for planning are organized around these three functions.

Investigating

Before a family sets out on a trip, it makes lists. It lists the places they are going to see, the things they must take, and the responsibilities of each member of the family. This process begins with a similar list, the "Overview of a Planning Process" (Figure 1). It articulates the critical points that a planning team must address. A good planning process addresses and answers each point in the "Overview" before moving on to the next.

Investigating, the first step in the overview, builds the foundation for future success. A pastoral plan will be only as effective as the information gathered in the early stages of the process allows it to be. With this in mind, planners begin by gathering two kinds of information. One kind of information is called "soft" information. This is information about the feelings, motives, hopes, dreams, and expectations of members of the parish. The other kind of information is "hard" data. This includes parish demographics and financial information. Both are important, but "soft" information—about the identity of the parish and its vision—is harder to get. Gathering and analyzing "hard" data, while necessary, is neither as complex nor as difficult.

Planners need not use all of the tools described in this chapter but they do need to answer all of the questions in the "Overview." Often, answers to more than one set of questions can be found by analyzing the results of one exercise several ways. The planning team should choose the tools or techniques that will best move the group forward, altering or adapting them to reflect the needs of the group or situation.

Figure 1

Overview of a Planning Process

TASK	QUESTIONS TO BE ANSWERED	EXERCISES
I. Investigating		
Identity	• What persons are involved in planning? What is our parish mission or purpose?	Who Plays Which Roles The Shape of the Community Memories of Church Appreciative Inquiry
Values	• What events, activities, programs, etc. are gaining life or growing and which are struggling or dying? Why? What motivates those involved?	Dying and Rising
Expectations	• What do those involved hope to accomplish? What changes do they dream of seeing?	Dream Trip
II. Considering		
Data analysis	• What material realities impact the situation? (demographics, economics, time, etc.)	Trend Analysis
Commitments	• What do those affected by parish programs expect the parish to accomplish?	Stakeholder Analysis
Brainstorming	• What actions could we take to address the situation and carry out our mission?	Brainstorming
Discerning	• What actions are most likely to achieve our purpose?	Prioritizing

Figure 1 continued on page 142

Figure 1 *continued from page 141*

Overview of a Planning Process

TASK	QUESTIONS TO BE ANSWERED	EXERCISES
III. **Recommending**		
Goals, Objectives	• How can we express the recommended actions as goals and objectives for those who will implement the plan?	Writing Goals & Objectives
Implementing	• Define tasks: What steps have to be taken to accomplish the actions? • Assign tasks: Who will be responsible for doing each of the actions? • Develop a Timeline: What is the timeframe for accomplishing the actions? • Evaluate: What are the criteria for success? When will the actions be evaluated?	Flow Chart
IV. Evaluating	• How effectively did we accomplish our goals? What did we learn? What might we change next time? What are our suggested next steps for moving forward?	

Each of the exercises described below takes approximately one hour to do if small numbers of people are involved. Two hours should be allowed for the exercise if large numbers of people are involved.

The first step, "investigating," involves three kinds of activities. They help the parish to clarify its identity, values, and expectations. The first tools are those that clarify the parish's identity.

Parish Identity

The first question, "What persons are involved in planning?" is answered by the composition of the planning team as previously discussed. The first thing the planning team does is clarify the roles each will play in the planning process. Fr. George Wilson's exercise, shown in Figure 3: "Who Plays Which Roles? And How?" in Chapter Four, is an easy way to accomplish this step.

The next questions help the planning team discover the parish's sense of mission or purpose. The planning team asks these additional questions: Who are we? What is our history? What is our purpose or mission? What personalities are involved in developing and carrying out the plan? No group can ever address all of these questions perfectly but they need to be considered carefully and seriously as the foundations of the planning process.

I once worked with a mission church that was too new to have developed a history or formed relationships. The planning team invited the entire membership of the mission to a meeting to discuss building a worship space for the community. At the meeting, I used a Management Design Institute exercise called "Memories of Church." This begins by asking each person to reflect on his or her earliest memories of being in church. They were to recall the clearest details they could about their memory, including where the incident took place, who was present, what time of day it occurred, and what smells, sounds, tastes, and feelings they remembered. Then I asked them to share their experiences in small groups. The groups discussed how these early memories continue to influence the way they feel about their membership in the church.

Out of this conversation, the group reported their insights on belonging to and being active members of their community. This helped them connect their memories with their life and mission as Christians and clarify their hopes for the worship space that they wanted to build. This exercise helped the parishioners project their feelings of connection to the church into their plans for the new worship space.

One of the first things a new parish pastoral council often does is to develop a parish mission statement. Depending on how it is done, this can effectively build a sense of identity. A parish mission statement that describes how the individual parish will uniquely carry out the general mission of the church can be crafted at any time. But planning does not have to wait until a formal mission statement is written. The church has a clear commission in Matthew 28:19–20, the mandate to bring the entire world to knowledge of salvation and to baptism. This commission can be a basis for good planning. It can be abbreviated to say, "Our mission is to proclaim the Good News of Jesus, the Christ, to the world." The most important thing is to begin with a sense of purpose.

A parish's identity and vision may be refined in a number of ways. One way described by George Wilson in Chapter Four is to invite parishioners to draw images of their parish. After the drawings are complete, parishioners can talk about how their drawings help them to understand the character, identity, and mission of the parish community. They can then share these insights with the whole group. The insights may be recorded on a piece of large paper and posted in a place visible to all, or a recorder may write them on a flip chart as they are called out. This exercise helps parishioners express their feelings freely, without prompting them to use one specific concept or another.

Another of George Wilson's exercises asks parishioners to describe what the parish was like when they joined it, and what the parish is like now. A third exercise reconstructs major events in the life of the parish as a framework for discussion. In using either of these exercises for planning the facilitator asks everyone present to look for common perceptions and to consider what they say about the special identity of this community. What areas of energy, life, or growth can be identified in the community? What areas of lack of energy, apathy, or resistance can be identified? What challenges for the community can we discover? How can we emphasize and build on those things that give life? George Wilson describes these exercises further in Chapter Four of this book. They help parishioners articulate the parish's identity and vision.

Another way to discover the parish's identity and vision is to stimulate a discussion about what people value in the parish, and what can strengthen those values. This is the Appreciative Inquiry approach taken by David DeLambo and Richard Krivanka in Chapter Five. It too is a powerful way to begin a planning process involving many parishioners.

Planning teams should adapt any of these exercises as they see fit. They can design questions to analyze the insights in a way that will be useful. For instance, a large group of parishioners writing a mission statement may generate a number of comments. Then the question for analysis might be, "Which comments do you feel are most helpful in describing the mission of the community?" The comments would be listed and incorporated into a draft of a mission statement. In all of these ways, planning teams can collect the hard-to-get "soft" information about the parish.

Planning teams also gather "hard" data about the parish. Good research, getting the facts about the situation, including information about available resources and current trends, is critical to effective planning. The U.S. Census is an especially good source of parish data, as George Cobb shows in Chapter Six. Teams should collect the following kinds of hard data:

- Parish statistics for each of the last three to five years (the planning group can use numbers submitted by the diocese for the *Official Catholic Directory*), including new registrations, the number of children enrolled in parish religious education, and sacramental records;
- Parish financial records for the last three to five years, including parish monthly income from collections and other sources, budget projections, and actual parish expenses;
- Demographic trends from the city, school districts, public utilities, chambers of commerce, or other sources, including population trends from the U.S. Census;
- Parish survey information, if available.

These data help parishioners to see the reality of the parish in an objective way. Parochial, financial, and demographic statistics complement and clarify the feelings of parishioners.

Sometimes parishioners resist the kinds of group exercises associated with this phase of planning. Resistance usually comes from uncertainty about what will be accomplished and concern about wasting people's time. But people need to take time in the early stages of planning to share their thoughts and feelings. They need to talk about the present situation, about their feelings associated with church, about their hopes and dreams, and perhaps about the history they share. Group exercises build energy, trust, and understanding—valuable resources for a group beginning to plan.

Parish Values

The planning team clarifies the values of a parish as well as its identity. Questions such as "What events, programs, activities, etc., are gaining life or growing and which are struggling or dying? Why?" and "What motivates those involved?" all invite people to share their perceptions about the parish. Often, planners find, people's perceptions differ but it is important to name the differences so that they can be discussed. The "Dying and Rising" exercise (Figure 2) helps people to name their perceptions of parish life.

Figure 2

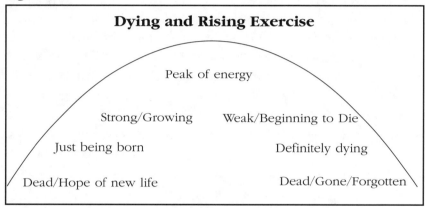

Dying and Rising Exercise

Peak of energy

Strong/Growing   Weak/Beginning to Die

Just being born   Definitely dying

Dead/Hope of new life   Dead/Gone/Forgotten

The "Dying and Rising" exercise begins with the facilitator's drawing a large curve on newsprint or on a black board. The curve represents a spectrum. At one end of the spectrum are the words "Dead/Hope of new life." At the other end of the spectrum are the words "Dead/Gone/Forgotten." At the top of the curve are the words "Peak of energy." With this curve before the parishioners, the facilitator invites them to name parish activities and where they go on the curve. Some activities are just beginning, gaining life, or growing. These are listed on the rising side of the curve. Others are struggling or dying. They are listed on the descending side of the curve. Activities that are in the peak of energy are written at the very top.

The facilitator makes it clear that the group is looking for people's perceptions about the life of the community. There are no right or wrong answers. If people disagree about where to locate a particular activity on the curve, the facilitator notes the disagreement and writes the activity in both places. The very fact that perceptions about parish life differ is an indication that people are dealing honestly with the process.

Some people will describe one parish program as being in the prime of life, while others are totally unaware of it. For example, in one parish a parishioner described adoration of the Blessed Sacrament as totally dead. Another parishioner experienced this devotion as a vital part of the life of the parish. Usually parish religious education and training of liturgical ministers are flourishing programs in parishes. But in some parishes these practices lack the energy they need to thrive. All of this is important information for a parish planning team.

Once parish events, activities, and programs are located on the curve, the group can analyze them. The facilitator asks why the things on the rising side of the curve are gaining life and energy and why the things on the descending side of the curve are struggling. This indicates what is giving or promoting life, the flow of God's grace, and an active sense of God's presence in this community. Deeper questioning can reveal to the group the values that motivate parishioners to get involved.

Generally, people share their time, talent, and treasure in the hope of making a difference. They volunteer because they hope to have an immediate, demonstrable effect on society. They want to make the world and their parish a better place. Planning that taps into these motivating values has a ready-made source of energy and a good chance of success.

Parish Expectations

To encourage involvement in parish life, planners need to discover parishioners' hopes and dreams by asking these questions: "What do those involved hope to accomplish?" "What changes do they dream of seeing?" This helps parishioners articulate their dreams for the future— how things could be. This lays the groundwork for a later task, namely, the development of activities, programs, and events that will make those dreams become reality.

I once worked with an inner-city, predominantly Hispanic parish that wanted to plan a new building. The parish had both a parochial school and a religious education program with more than 1,000 students. Because resources were limited, the parish and the school needed to share the new building. This would require maximizing the value of the building for both the schoolchildren and the other parishioners.

In order to clarify the expectations of the parish, I invited the parishioners to take a "dream trip." Using a "Dream Trip Worksheet" (Figure 3), the participants formed a number of small groups. Members individually recorded their dreams for the parish. Then they shared the dreams with their group. Finally, each group identified the dreams most commonly expressed by the members.

As it worked through the results of this exercise, the planning team came to realize several things. First, the architecture of the new building needed to embody the parish's Hispanic identity. Second, because of the school's historic importance to the neighborhood, the nearly 100-year-old main school building would have to remain the centerpiece of the campus. And, finally, the new building would need to be very flexible to satisfy the needs of all the groups that would be using it. The dream trip worksheet was a vital beginning point for the design of the new facility. It helped people articulate their individual dreams and integrate those dreams into a larger dream for the community.

Considering

The planning process begins by investigating the parish's identity, sense of mission, and values and expectations. The next step in the planning process is "considering." In this step the planning team sifts through the information they have gathered and analyzes it from a variety of perspectives. Then the planning team imagines possibilities for future action.

The work of considering falls under four headings. One is data analysis. It enables the planning team to spot trends. The second focuses on the mandates or commitments of key people in the parish community. The third is the creative task of generating possibilities through the process of brainstorming. The final heading is discerning. Once a planning team has analyzed the data, reflected on the community's commitments, and creatively brainstormed a number of possibilities, then it must discern what is best for the parish.

Figure 3

Dream Trip Worksheet

1. Personal: Dreams I have for my church

    List three   Why they are important to me: Why they are important for my church:

  a.

  b.

  c.

2. Other dreams developed by members of my small group:

3. Small group report: Those dreams chosen by my small group as the ones most commonly valued:

  a.

  b.

  c.

Source: Management Design Institute/George B. Wilson, S.J.

Data Analysis

In a planning journey with the parish, we have seen that the first task is to clarify the identity of the parish. Sharing memories of the church, developing a mission statement, and doing an Appreciative Inquiry are three ways to capture the parish's sense of identity. The next step is acquiring demographic information—"hard data"—such as parish statistics, financial records, and demographic information. These are also critical ways of describing the parish. Hard data answers the question: "What material realities impact the situation?"

Acquiring and analyzing data are technical aspects of planning that require a different set of skills than other aspects. In Chapters Three and Seven, Marian Schwab and John Flaherty pointed out the need to have people whose interests and skills complement one another. Nothing makes clearer the tension between the spiritual/pastoral and practical/technical sides of planning than dealing with numbers. A "Trend Analysis" is an easy way for planning teams to reconcile this tension while analyzing hard data.

A Trend Analysis aims at making an educated guess about the future of the parish. It can involve many people. When a Trend Analysis exercise involves more than twelve or fifteen people, small groups are formed to deal with each area of interest. Participants identify their interests by category, such as sociological, economic, pastoral, educational, or "other" (participants decide what they want to put in this last category). Each small group examines the hard data and makes its best guess about what the parish will be like in three to five years. A worksheet can be developed to stimulate thinking. Typical statements on the worksheet would be:

Sociological Trends:
- Parish membership will (grow, shrink, stay the same).
- The median age will (increase, decrease, stay the same).
- This will affect parish programs (how?).
- The ethnic composition will (change, stay the same) in (these ways).
- This will have (effect) on parish life.

Economic Trends:
- The median family income will (increase, decrease, stay the same).
- The budget of (parish or organization) will (grow, shrink, stay the same).
- Economic demands (on the parish/organization) will (grow, shrink, stay the same) in (these ways).

Pastoral Trends:
- Ministry to (youth, the aged, the poor, the sick or homebound, etc.) will (grow, diminish, etc.) in (these ways).

Educational Trends:
- The need for (adult, family, Catholic school, sacrament preparation, etc.) will (increase, decrease, stay the same).

Other Trends:
- Parish staff (paid, volunteer) will (grow, shrink, stay the same).
- Money paid in salaries and benefits will (increase, decrease, stay the same).

People like doing this exercise because they can easily see its value for planning. They might be a little uncomfortable about guessing, thinking that their guesses might not be valid. They can be assured that they know their community as well as anybody can and their guesses are as good as anybody's. Of course, the unexpected can happen as industries move out, population changes, or new ethnic groups move in. Some of these things can be predicted while others are a surprise. Surprises do not invalidate the plan. Having a plan will make the parish more sensitive to changes, and the plan can be adjusted as necessary during a scheduled evaluation.

Other data might be useful in planning. Depending on the thrust or focus of planning, information regarding attitudes might be valuable. For instance, a possible capital campaign could be preceded by a feasibility study that questions a number of parishioners about their feelings regarding the project and their support of it. Likewise, a full attitudinal survey (including Appreciative Inquiry interviews or survey) might accompany the development of a five-year plan.

Commitments

Considering or reflecting on the future of the parish is most productive when looked at from several points of view. Parishes have commitments beyond the parishioners. Canon 529.2, for example, states that pastors have an explicit obligation to exercise care over non-parishioners within the territory. Many non-parishioners have a stake in the parish because they live within its boundaries or because it has an impact on their lives. It may be helpful, and in some cases necessary, to analyze their expectations for the parish and its plan. Using a "Stakeholder Analysis Worksheet" (Figure 4) can be helpful in considering how the parish or organization looks from the point of view of others. It invites planners to examine the parish's relations to its non-parishioner stakeholders, what the parish needs from them, and their importance to the parish. A stakeholder analysis helps planners to answer the question: "What do those affected by parish programs expect the parish to accomplish?"

I once did a "Stakeholder Analysis" with the executive board of the Social Services Ministry of an urban parish. The board members were aware that, from the point of view of most parishioners and contributors, they were doing a wonderful job. However, from the point of view of the clients, especially food bank recipients, the ministry was in trouble. In the tense and unhappy atmosphere volunteer hours were falling off and personality clashes were increasing, threatening the survival of the ministry. The Stakeholder Analysis exercise helped to locate and clarify the most troubled areas. Addressing the problems in the food bank required training for nearly a hundred volunteers. The ministry's mission and the procedures and policies of the food bank were reviewed and updated. Renewed commitment to shared values began to ensure an efficient, dependable process of food distribution. One year from the day they began planning, this previously troubled ministry was attracting new volunteers and more happily satisfying its clients and long-time supporters.

Figure 4

Stakeholder Analysis Worksheet

Instructions: For each stakeholder listed fill out a separate Analysis Worksheet

Stakeholder:			
Criteria Used by Stakeholder To Assess Our Performance	Our Sense of Their Judgment About Our Performance		
	Very good	Okay	Poor

How does this Stakeholder relate to us?

What do we need from this Stakeholder?

How important is this Stakeholder?

_____ Extremely

_____ Reasonably

_____ Not very

_____ Not at all

Brainstorming

At this stage, planners have gathered information, analyzed data, and examined their commitments. Brainstorming is a productive next step. Brainstorming generates possible responses to the data gathered. It asks, "What actions could we take to address the situation and carry out our mission?"

Brainstorming allows participants in a planning process to respond to the results of the investigation. It lets people imagine possibilities for the parish in a creative and spontaneous way. It can be fun and energizing if the group allows ideas to flow freely.

In brainstorming, the facilitator states a question for the planning group to consider. The facilitator reminds the group that there are no wrong answers and that all ideas are good ideas. Giving individuals a few moments of quiet time to jot down their initial thoughts is the first step. Next, participants form small groups of two to four members. The small group members put all of the individuals' ideas together and add any new ideas that occur to them. Then the small groups submit their ideas to the whole group. The facilitator writes all of the ideas on newsprint or poster paper. When necessary, the ideas can be clarified and gathered into categories. After the group has generated a number of possible responses to the planning situation, it evaluates them. This moves the group into the next phase, that of discerning.

Discerning

Discerning, weighing the results of an investigation, lies at the very heart of planning for the parish's future. When all of the information has been gathered and analyzed, and after the planning team has brainstormed possible responses, planners ask, "What actions are most likely to achieve our purpose?" Planners must select from the possibilities. No person, parish, or diocese can do everything, although some seem to try. Limited resources (financial, personnel, time, energy, etc.) dictate choosing among various goods. Sometimes, the choice is so obvious that there is almost no feeling of having chosen. More often, making a choice is difficult.

A rule of thumb in planning states that no more than three ideas or endeavors can claim a parish's attention at any one time. Simply maintaining the parish is always a priority in order to assure its viability. After maintaining itself, the parish can effectively accomplish, at most, two other things. Choosing one priority and addressing it successfully is better than choosing several and failing at any.

The planning team develops its priorities in a process of discernment. Discernment is a form of spirituality that seeks to know the will of God in a particular situation. The planning team prays that the Holy Spirit will grant it wisdom to sort through the possibilities and to choose a future direction. This is best accomplished in an atmosphere like that of the upper room, where Jesus and his disciples celebrated the Last Supper, as described by Loughlan Sofield in Chapter Two. Priorities discerned in a spiritual atmosphere are more likely to capture the allegiance and energy of the parish.

Prioritizing can be a simple process. The first step is to post all of the possible courses of action in a place where everyone can see them. Second, the team discusses each course thoroughly making sure that each person's point of view is clearly understood. As part of this thorough discussion, all of the negative aspects of a certain course of action could be brainstormed and listed on newsprint. Then, all of the positive aspects could be brainstormed and listed. A "prioritizing exercise" is the final step in the discernment process.

A prioritizing exercise is a way to get each member of the planning team to express a preference for various courses of action. The list of possible courses of action is placed where everyone can reach it. Then each member receives any number (three to five is usual) of adhesive dots (available at any office supply store). Each team member puts the dots on the items he or she prefers. All of an individual's dots can be placed on one course of action, or the dots can be divided any way he or she likes. Those courses of action receiving the largest number of dots are the top priorities for the group. People enjoy this process because everyone participates equally and the results are clear.

Occasionally, if the situation is complicated or the choices are difficult, a planning team may desire a more refined prioritizing exercise. A refined prioritizing exercise is adjusted to allow participants to weigh their preference for a particular course of action according to priorities. This may be most clearly illustrated by describing an actual case study.

One day I was invited to assist a parish director of religious education and the leadership of the parish religious education program. They worked in a large, culturally diverse, inner-city parish. The members felt completely overwhelmed by their situation. They felt that they had more problems than remedies and more projects than resources.

First the group listed all of the activities, programs, and events that involved the parish school of religion. Next, they identified who was responsible for each thing, they evaluated the work involved in accomplishing it, and they rated its effectiveness. Then they listed all of the programs, events, and activities that they dreamed of starting, and they named who might take responsibility for them. All current and possible future projects were listed on chart paper and posted on the wall. Finally, without getting into budget details, they discussed available resources.

Once they had described their situation and articulated their dreams, the religious education leaders brainstormed ways to improve their situation. They listed eight or nine possibilities that were then sifted through a refined prioritizing exercise. The leaders considered, first, which improvement would be most effective, second, which improvement they had the resources to implement, and, third, which improvement was most urgently needed. Each of the leaders chose three possible improvements, ranking them in order of importance and assigning each a number. A three indicated the *most* important improvement; a one indicated the *least* important.

When the scores were tallied, the top priority was perfectly clear. Another item was a distant second. All other possible responses were so far behind that they could safely be discarded. The prioritizing exercise was a huge comfort because they had worked successfully together to achieve a consensus on where to spend their energies for the best effect.

Recommending

Thus far, the planning process has investigated the parish's identity, mission, and values. Next, it has considered possible courses of action. The final step in planning is recommending.

The final task of the planning team is to report its findings to those who will decide which courses of action will be pursued. In the case of a parish pastoral council this is the pastor. In the first stages of recommendation the planning team should take time to be creative with possibilities, generating many possible courses of action. They should not settle too quickly for one possibility and become advocates for it. A planning team would be wise to remember that it is not the only group consulted by the pastor. Others may influence the pastor's decisions.

As explained earlier, clarity about roles should be established at the beginning of the planning process. The role of a parish pastoral council is to assist in fostering the pastoral activity of the parish. If the pastor has been part of the planning process, recommending and decision making will be a seamless process.

A planning team does not always implement its own recommendations. Once the pastor has accepted them, others (such as the pastoral staff, ministerial commissions, or committees of volunteers) may be charged with implementation. If this is the case, implementers could be consulted in the planning process. Including them will ensure that the plans are realistic and that the implementers are enthusiastic about carrying them out.

After a certain course of action has been chosen, the implementers participate in establishing goals and objectives.

Goals and Objectives

As with analyzing hard data, tension may exist between the spiritual/pastoral function of the council and the practical/technical function of planning. Each council, in consultation with the pastor and exercising discernment in the call of the Holy Spirit, has to work these things out in the best way for the unique parish community it serves. With this in mind, goals and objectives may direct the implementation of the pastoral plan. A goal is a general description of what the group intends to achieve within a given time (such as three years). Goals should be specific and concrete. "We will get more people involved," is a poor goal because it is not specific. A better statement is, "Our goal is to increase participation in a particular program by ten percent in the next six months."

An objective is a concrete, goal-oriented action taken within a specific time frame. An objective indicates the specific action, identifies who will execute it, clarifies to what extent it should be done, and states the time by which the action will be achieved. If the example is the goal of increasing participation in a program by 10%, a list of objectives to accomplish this goal might be:

- Each person currently involved will invite one other person to come to a meeting on September 27.

- Fliers will be put in the bulletin on September 6 and 13, outlining the purpose and accomplishments of the organization and inviting people to attend an information meeting on September 27. John Smith will design and print the fliers, and Mary Jones will arrange for the ushers to insert them in the bulletins.

- An article about the organization and its history with quotations from current members will be published in the parish newsletter on September 15. Samantha Goforth will gather the information and write the article.

- All members will be prepared to welcome and orient new members at the September 27 meeting. Tasks will be clearly described and current members will be assigned to assist new members in accomplishing these tasks.

Implementing
Planning is a waste of time if nothing happens as a result. Even though the planning team, *per se*, is not the group that will actually implement the plan, it shares responsibility for assuring that implementation will take place. It does this by gathering, empowering, and energizing those persons, committees, groups, or organizations that will be involved in the implementation.

Implementation includes defining the tasks, assigning people to accomplish them, developing a timeline, and evaluating accomplishment. Planners can use a flow chart (Figure 5) to assist with implementation. The flow chart helps to state the expectations for each objective. No plan is finished until everyone knows who will do what by when. The planning team should take an active role in this phase of implementation.

Figure 5

Flow Chart

Goal/Objective to be achieved:

What steps will be taken to achieve this goal/objective?	Who will be responsible for this step?	When is this step to be completed?	What resources will be needed for this step?	What will the result of this step be?

Evaluating

Clear goals and concrete objectives make evaluation easy. Evaluation is the last step in the planning process. In one sense, evaluation may be the most important step because it measures the success of the plan. Even if nothing else is accomplished, a good evaluation can assure that the planning team learns from its lack of success.

Conclusion

There is no reason, however, to anticipate a lack of success. Good planning is meant to ensure success. When a family plans a vacation, it does so to ensure that the vacation is comfortable, stimulating, and life-giving. Parish planning is meant to do the same. A SMART plan will succeed.

SPECIFIC (with clearly articulated goals and objectives),

MEASURABLE (with concrete, quantifiable goals and objectives),

ACHIEVABLE (with goals that are clearly within the abilities of the members),

RELEVANT TO MISSION (built upon the parish's mission or purpose), and

TIME RELATED (describing a time frame for accomplishment).

Just like a family planing a vacation trip, a parish is wise to plan for its future. Planning can stimulate a renewed sense of mission and purpose. The planning process can be a fun, energizing, exciting, happy time for the planning team as well as for the parish. Planning offers opportunities to learn about others, to express ideas, to dream of better times, and to come more deeply and truly in touch with the work of the Holy Spirit. It is well worth the effort.

CHAPTER NINE

Sharing More Than a Pastor

Mary Montgomery

In the 1950s the Archdiocese of Dubuque had more priests per Catholic than any other diocese in the United States. This ratio began to change in the 1960s when the number of priests began to fall dramatically. On average, 40 fewer priests were available to serve the archdiocese every five years in the 1980s and 1990s. Researchers predicted that, by 2005, the number of active priests in the archdiocese would decline by more than 70% from the number in 1965.[1] By the early 1990s this prediction was proving true. The Archdiocese of Dubuque recognized that it had a serious challenge.

The decline in the number of priests was first felt in parishes when the archdiocese began to assign a single pastor to multiple parishes. By 1992 almost two-thirds of parishes were sharing a pastor. Several parishes had closed. The strain on pastors' energies caused by the inefficiency of then-current methods of managing multiple parishes called for a new style of management. Pressure for change and John Paul II's exhortation for renewal of the whole church in preparation for the Jubilee Year provided the impetus for planning in the archdiocese.

The basis for the creation of new structures begins with Vatican II. In addition to allowing the establishment of diocesan and parish councils, the documents of Vatican II suggest the possibility of other structures to serve the church. The "Decree on the Apostolate of the Laity" (no. 26) mentions councils at the "parochial, inter-parochial [and] inter-diocesan level...." These councils are to "assist the church's apostolic work" and "take care of the mutual coordinating of the various lay associations and undertakings."[2] In other words, Vatican II envisioned the possibility of new structures operating at all levels of church life and apostolic activity.

Faced with challenging circumstances, the Archdiocese of Dubuque has responded, in part, by creating new structures. More than a reaction to perceived crisis, these structures are the result of a thoughtful, gospel-focused process of discovery, clarification, and goal-setting. The challenge for parishes to collaborate in sharing pastoral programs and resources has fostered new and creative pastoral life in the parishes. New structures provide a foundation for developing vital communities of faith in all parishes, including those without a resident priest. The experience of Dubuque in working through this process can serve as a model both for other dioceses and for parishes that seek to use their resources more efficiently and effectively.

The Planning Process

Decreased numbers of priests is not the only significant challenge for the church of the future. Threats to families, concerns for youth, and a need for competent lay leadership, among other things, also face the church at the parish, diocesan, and universal levels. An effective planning process invites the people to identify the challenges and to suggest ways to address them. Planning gives people an opportunity to reflect on their situation and to pool their resources. Knowing this, in 1995 Archbishop Jerome Hanus initiated a strategic planning process. This process has resulted in many parishes forming clusters, sharing resources, and cooperating with one another to employ staff and plan for the future. Today, pastors are less harried and parishioners feel more empowered and responsible. Although clustered parishes are still in transition, they seem to offer a model for inter-parochial cooperation.

Church planning is not an abstract exercise but a response to concrete pastoral needs. Planning is a search for good answers to difficult questions, a method of drawing upon the wisdom of the Catholic community, and a process of consultation that builds commitment to a better future. The planning process used by the Archdiocese of Dubuque can help parish pastoral councils see and understand the value of planning.

The Pastoral Situation

Planning begins with a good grasp of current reality. In 1995, the Archbishop of Dubuque, acting on the recommendation of the archdiocesan pastoral council, the priests' council, and the board of education, established a planning task force. The focus of this task force was revitalization of the local church. The task force agreed from the beginning that in moving toward the future the Archdiocese of Dubuque "will be a Roman Catholic community of believers, shaped primarily by the gospel, but also by the Catholic theological tradition, especially as this is expressed in Vatican II and in subsequent documents of the church."

The first action of the task force was to invite participation by the people of the archdiocese. Nine hundred and sixty parish pastoral council members were trained to conduct speak-out meetings in their parishes. Over 11,000 parishioners participated in the meetings to name the challenges the church faced in the new millennium. Four areas of strategic concern emerged from these meetings: parish life (community), education, leadership, and family.

Vision 2000: A Vision and Plan for the Archdiocese of Dubuque in the Twenty-First Century, based on these concerns, formed the framework for the subsequent planning process. Figure 1 (page 164) is the vision statement from *Vision 2000*. *Vision 2000* articulates the vision and values the archdiocese carried forward in the planning process. *Vision 2000* commits the people of the archdiocese to developing "vital communities of faith in all parishes, including those without a resident pastor." The archdiocese then developed resources to enable parishes to carry out this commitment.

Figure 1

Vision 2000
Archdiocese of Dubuque

We envision . . .

This faith and these principles inspire us to envision a church in which we

- are disciples of Christ, empowered by the Holy Spirit to be a **community** devoted to the apostles' instruction and the communal life, to the breaking of bread and the prayers, zealous in caring for the needs of others. (Acts 1:8; 2:42; 4:34)

- are people in whom the biblical **Word of God** finds rich soil, flourishes in the truth of Catholic theology, and produces a harvest of holiness and social justice. (Luke 6:45; 8:8)

- are ministered to by faith-filled and qualified **persons in leadership** who imitate the Good Shepherd and are "worthy of their hire." (1 Peter 5:1–4; Mt 10:10)

- support **families**, in various forms, striving to be domestic churches that instill Catholic faith and morality in the hearts of the next generation. (Ephesians 5:31–6:4)

The Cluster Planning Process

The second step in planning is imagining and developing creative responses to current realities. Given current realities in Dubuque, simply assigning pastors to multiple parishes would not be sufficient to develop "vital communities of faith." The situation clearly called for parishes to cooperate with one another in imaginative new ways. Inter-parochial cooperation could be facilitated by new structures: parish clusters.

With the strong support of archdiocesan advisory councils, a plan to assist parishes in moving into clusters was developed by a cluster task force composed of episcopal vicars, priests, deacons, laity, and a theologian. This plan includes guidelines for developing parish clusters. The plan and guidelines maximize the efficient use of parish resources and personnel.

The story of Father Clayton Landherr illustrates some of the issues faced by parish clusters. Father Landherr is a young priest in his first pastorate. He serves a cluster of five rural parishes totaling almost 500 families. With him is Msgr. Thomas Ralph, a retired pastor who retains his position as editor of the archdiocesan newspaper. The two priests rotate the schedule of Masses, with Msgr. Ralph celebrating two Masses on the weekend.

The liturgical and sacramental life of the parish is crucial. Parish vitality depends on it, and leaders must provide it. This requires a number of decisions, for example, about where and when Masses will be celebrated. In Father Landherr's cluster, representatives from each parish developed the Mass schedule.

After the first six months of being pastor of this cluster of parishes, Father Landherr gave this report:

> Msgr. Ralph has said that, for him, it's tough getting from 8:00 A.M. Mass at St John's to the 9:30 A.M. Mass at St. Lawrence when he covers both. Initially, I did try to offer daily Mass twice weekly at both Assumption and St. Theresa's, in addition to daily Mass at Holy Rosary. However, I have dropped the daily Mass at St. Theresa's due to poor attendance.

When a pastor is responsible for multiple parishes, he quickly learns that he must adjust his style of ministry. He is challenged to make effective use of his and other staff members' time. In evaluating his cluster, Father Landherr had this to say:

> Liturgically and sacramentally, the cluster Mass schedule that the council initially put together has seemed acceptable. Both Msgr. Ralph and I have noticed increased freedom on the part of people to attend Mass at any of the cluster parishes, depending on which is most convenient for them on a given weekend.

The cluster pastoral planning process enables individual parishes to describe how they would cooperate with one another by, for example, developing job descriptions for joint staff positions and setting goals to guide the cluster beyond the first year.

The cluster pastoral planning process sets parameters for the cluster and criteria for parish cooperation and describes how parishes are formed into clusters. Parishes are given room to be creative in designing the agreement for making joint decisions. No two clusters are exactly alike. Their cluster agreements reflect the struggle to plan cooperatively for the future growth of all.

A cluster is defined in terms of collaboration to share pastoral leadership, staff, resources, and programs. The goal of clustering is to ensure that parishes have sufficient resources, now and in the future, to support a vibrant and vital faith community without placing unrealistic expectations or undue burdens on the pastor, staff, or parishioners. Clustering enables parishes to coordinate ministerial activities more effectively.

Collaboration within the cluster promotes a sharing of parish life, resources, and programs. It fosters a sense of community within the parishes of the cluster and the archdiocesan church. Each parish retains its unique character, structures, and functions, including a pastoral council and a finance council. In addition, a new cluster council, composed of representatives from each of the cluster's parishes, is established to address the cluster's special concerns and to plan for the growth of the whole.

Parameters for Clustering

Having defined what the archdiocese hoped to accomplish with parish clustering, the task force then expressed how clustering would be accomplished. Parameters for clustering were published in archdiocesan cluster guidelines. The first parameter says that, whenever possible, no priest would celebrate Mass more than three times on a weekend. Four Masses is the absolute limit set by the archdiocese, even if this means that some parishes would not have Mass every weekend. The cluster guidelines require every parish cluster to design a workable schedule of Masses.

The guidelines describe expectations of the cluster's professional staff. "Professional staff" might mean a pastoral associate, a director of religious education, or a business manager. In some parishes, day-to-day administration might be the responsibility of a person other than the priest. The responsibilities and qualifications of the staff would vary but each cluster must have at least one professional assistant to the pastor.

The guidelines also clarify budgeting procedures. In addition to each parish budget, the cluster must also develop a cluster budget that distributes the cost of shared services, programs, and personnel among the parishes. In summary, the guidelines encourage cooperation and collaboration among the parishes in a cluster.

Each individual parish must be committed to the success of the cluster. This often requires a significant level of change on the part of all involved. Parish leaders provide vision, accountability, networking, and faith in the process. Parishioners are called on to adjust to new Mass schedules and increased financial obligations to cover the cost of additional staff. Even the archdiocese is challenged to alter policies to reflect new realities.

The Clustering Process

The value of planning is realized in implementation—in this case, forming a cluster. Often, implementation requires more time and is more complicated than planning. Also, implementation usually involves going over much of the same ground traveled in planning, only with different people. Implementation justifies the time spent in planning; without implementation, planning is a waste of time. The clustering process undertaken by the Archdiocese of Dubuque illustrates the time, patience, and resources required to implement a plan.

The clustering process has two parts: choosing parishes to form a cluster and helping the parishes come together and reach agreement on how they will collaborate.

Choosing Parishes to Cluster

Father Landherr's cluster of parishes is an example of how this process works. The parishes of St. John, St. Lawrence, Assumption, St. Theresa, and Holy Rosary are in a rural area of the Archdiocese of Dubuque. Their proximity suggested them as candidates for clustering.

The process began with a meeting of the episcopal vicar and the dean of the rural area in which the parishes are located. The episcopal vicar is appointed by the archbishop to oversee a particular geographical area. The dean is a priest appointed by the archbishop with responsibilities and rights for a specific number of parishes in a geographic area. In

Dubuque, deans are accountable to the archbishop through the episcopal vicar. The archbishop meets monthly with the vicars to discuss such
issues as proposed clustering. Implementation of plans to cluster is delegated to the episcopal vicars and the director of pastoral planning. The
episcopal vicar and dean met to determine which parishes to invite into
a conversation that could lead to clustering.

A number of factors are considered in selecting parishes for clustering, including such things as: age of pastor, length of pastoral assignment, anticipated population shifts, and a need for a new church due to
population growth. These particular five parishes were chosen because
several pastors in the area were about to retire and one pastoral assignment was coming to a close.

Once they identified parishes that were likely to form a cluster, the
episcopal vicar and dean met with the director of pastoral planning and
the pastors of the selected parishes. The clustering process was
described, and the leadership role of the pastors was clarified.

Together, the archdiocesan officials and the pastors considered how
ready the five parishes were for clustering, articulating both the problems and opportunities they could foresee in such a relationship. One
advantage they could see immediately was a strengthening of religious
education in the five parishes. One major concern was how parishioners
would feel about changes in the Sunday and daily Mass schedules.

Finally, the archdiocesan officials and the pastors met with the parish
councils, interested parishioners, and the staff of the five parishes. The
goal of clustering was explained, concerns were explored, and the
readiness of the five parishes for clustering was considered. The councillors and pastors expressed their willingness to go forward.

Responsibility for a five-parish cluster can be awesome, especially for
a young priest. Father Landherr described his feelings about this meeting to other priests:

> I knew that I was ready to become a pastor and hoped the archdiocese
> would assign me to a small rural parish and, after a few years, I would be
> moved to a larger one. I soon learned that in the Archdiocese of Dubuque,
> "small rural parish" means two parishes. I was told "in three to five years
> we will begin a clustering process for the neighboring three parishes."

Then I learned that in Dubuque "three to five years" really means one and a half years! This was to be the first ever five-parish cluster in the archdiocese.

Being asked to care for the five-parish[3] cluster gave me a much stronger kinship to the disciples gathered in the upper room on the eve of Pentecost. My head and heart were filled with questions and some fear. I had no idea how I would go about this. What would I say to the people? How would I meet the challenge of bringing the five parishes into a collaborative working relationship? What if it didn't work?

As I met with the episcopal vicar, the director of pastoral planning and the parish councils of the five parishes, I realized in a new way what Pentecost and the coming of the Holy Spirit meant. As I watched the reaction of the laity and heard the answers to the questions that had been on my mind, I began to see that this could be done. Much to my surprise, I soon heard the words coming out of my mouth, "I think we can do this! I have a vision of how this can work."

Father Landherr realized that his vision alone would not direct the effort. The vision of the archbishop and archdiocesan authorities that had moved the process to this point and the vision of the laity working with him would also guide the parishes.

Forming a Cluster Planning Committee

Once the pastor and pastoral councils of the five rural parishes agreed to work toward clustering they informed all of the parishioners. Representatives of each of the parishes were chosen to serve on a cluster pastoral planning committee. This group would actually plan for the cluster. It had nine tasks:

1. Study specific issues that the plan for clustering should address;

2. Identify resources in each parish to support and sustain the mission of the church;

3. Identify and prioritize the strengths and limitations of the proposed cluster;

4. Keep parish councils and parishioners informed regarding cluster planning;

5. Develop a plan for the clustering process;

6. Develop a timetable for implementation;

7. Present the plan for clustering for the approval of the episcopal vicar and the archbishop;

8. Continue to work on implementation of the approved plan; and

9. Prepare reports on cluster progress.

Forming a cluster is a six-to-twelve month process requiring at least four to six meetings. Each meeting has a specific agenda described by the cluster guidelines so that significant progress will be made toward forming the cluster. Figure 2 shows the agenda for the first meeting. Detailed agendas demonstrate the level of archdiocesan support provided for the process. Pastors and parish representatives are expected to attend all cluster pastoral planning committee meetings.

Good communication is a key to relieving concerns about the future of the parishes. Periodic meetings held after Masses, bulletin announcements, and open meetings promote communication. The five parishes of Father Landherr's cluster followed all of these recommendations in their planning.

The cluster pastoral planning committee understood that its work was both consultative and part of a larger process. It was not the final decision maker. The plan for clustering was subject first, to acceptance by the parish councils of the parishes, then to the endorsement of the episcopal vicar and then, finally, to the approval of the archbishop.

The Cluster Planning Process

The cluster pastoral planning committee for Father Landherr's cluster completed its plan in five meetings. This involved the members reaching agreement on difficult issues. One concern was religious education in the cluster. The committee suggested ways to streamline the education programs and eliminate duplicated effort. After the cluster was formed, a newly hired staff person, Sister Virginia Crilly, B.V.M., acted on the committee's recommendations. Reflecting on this issue six months after the formation of the cluster, Father Landherr wrote:

Figure 2 (Sample Agenda)

FIRST MEETING
CLUSTER PASTORAL PLANNING COMMITTEE (CPPC)

Purpose:

> Introduce the cluster process
>
> Provide archdiocesan perspectives
>
> Identify first steps for parishes
>
> Initiate the *Parish Resource Study*
>
> Answer questions

Participants

Episcopal Vicar, Dean, Cluster Pastoral Planning Committee, Staff, Parish Councils, Director of Pastoral Planning

Agenda:

Welcome, Prayer and Introductions

Rationale for Clustering Process

Definition of a cluster

Experience of clustering in the Archdiocese of Dubuque

Reason for clustering now

> *Vision 2000* commitments—Community Goal 1.2
>
> Availability of priests and religious
>
> Vitality of parish life

Rationale for *this* grouping of parishes

Expectations of the dialogue among parishes

Sharing of parish studies, identifying strengths and limitations

Assessing staffing requirements

Affirming or adjusting the grouping of parishes

Developing a plan to implement clustering

Process

Appoint a chairperson and identify a secretary/communications person

Explain the structure of the committee

Give directions for the *Parish Resource Study*

Review cluster models

Develop a plan for *this* cluster

Describe the approval process

> Next meeting: Date _____ Place:_____Time:_____
>
> Prayer Leader:_____

Tasks to be completed by next meeting:

Parish Resource Study completed by each Parish Council or subcommittee

Pastors and Parish Councils share information regarding cluster process with their own parish, e.g., bulletin inserts and/or meeting minutes distributed to CPPC

Closing Prayer

It seems that some of our efforts to coordinate and consolidate certain aspects of our religious education programs have met with acceptance. These include a shared confirmation retreat for our young people and also a cluster-wide first reconciliation service. We hope to coordinate these programs more next year by following the same schedule and using the same curriculum and textbooks in each of our parishes.

A detailed overview of the five planning meetings shows what was accomplished in each meeting.

The First Meeting
The meeting took place in one of the five parishes and included representatives from each parish. The episcopal vicar presented archdiocesan perspectives, including the wise use of priestly resources and the need for cooperation among parishes. Some parishioners attending this meeting expressed their fear that the archdiocese already had a plan and that the committee would have little effect. The vicar acknowledged that, after clustering, a resident pastor would not be serving in each of the five parishes. Eventually, only one priest would serve the cluster, but Msgr. Ralph would help with weekend Masses as long as his health allowed. The vicar assured parishioners that the archbishop would rely on the cluster pastoral planning committee's insights in developing and implementing the clustering plan.

The director of pastoral planning presented the *Parish Resource Study* containing archdiocesan criteria for parish vitality to the cluster pastoral planning committee. Figure 3 is a page from the Parish Resource Study, showing the kinds of questions it asks. Six areas of parish life: spiritual growth (including liturgical practices), education, parish life, social concerns, finance, and administration/leadership are examined in the light of criteria for parish vitality. Members of the planning committee work with the parish councils of their parishes to prepare a report on each parish. These reports are presented at the next meeting of the Cluster Pastoral Planning Committee.

The parish report is not a way to identify good or bad parishes; it is simply a description of the current situation in each parish. As the planners work toward participation in a cluster, the report helps them iden-

Figure 3: Sample page from the Parish Resource Study [4]

PARISH RESOURCE STUDY
Criteria for Parish Vitality
SPIRITUAL GROWTH AND LITURGY

THE PARISH IS A WORSHIPING COMMUNITY THAT EXPRESSES AND DEVELOPS ITS RELATIONSHIP WITH GOD THROUGH LITURGICAL CELEBRATIONS.

Criterion #1

The Liturgy, particularly the Eucharist, is the central focus of the faith community and it is celebrated in the spirit and practice of Vatican II.

Y   N   a) A Director of Liturgy and Music is a part of our parish staff and has appropriate education, ability, and experience to enhance liturgical celebrations.

This person serves the parish:

_____Full time   _____Part-time
_____Paid salary/stipend   _____Volunteer
_____This person serves the liturgical needs of the parish as part of job responsibilities of another full-time position.

Y   N   b) Liturgy committee is involved in ongoing formation and provides formation opportunities for liturgical ministers and the assembly:

_____a committee regularly meets to do seasonal planning, prepare the liturgy and assess liturgical needs.

_____There are enough ministers for each Mass (lectors, eucharistic ministers, servers, musicians, ushers, etc.) to avoid duplicate functions at the same Mass.

_____Efforts are made to provide music that reflects the liturgical action and season.

Y   N   c) Weekday Mass or other liturgical celebrations:
_____ daily
_____ 3-5 times a week
_____ times a week

(Figure 3 continued on page 174)

Figure 3 (continued)

Y   N   d) When there is no Mass on weekdays, we have:

_____ Liturgy of the Hours   _____ Liturgy of the Word
_____ Communion Service   _____ No service

Y   N   e) The schedule of Sunday Masses is re-evaluated based on attendance numbers and availability of priest.

Y   N   f) Environment appropriate to the liturgical season is provided in the worship space.

Y   N   g) We need to renovate our worship space according to the norms of Vatican II.

Y   N   h) We have an art/environment team to work with the liturgy committee.

Y   N   i) We have special liturgies with children and use the Lectionary designed for them.

Y   N   j) Provisions are made to welcome and include persons with special needs.
We provide:
_____ Wheelchair accessibility   _____Listening devices
_____ Large print missalettes   _____ Greeters to assist those
                                                 needing help

(The parish resource study is available from the Archdiocese of Dubuque, Office of Pastoral Planning, P.O. Box 479, Dubuque, IA 52004-0479)

---

tify and prioritize issues of common concern. When the cluster is ready to hire professional staff, the report serves as a basis for writing job descriptions and deciding which positions to fill first.

After the first meeting, members of the cluster pastoral planning committee were better informed about their role. And writing the parish resource report was a clear task to accomplish before the next meeting.

The Second Meeting

Several weeks later the cluster pastoral planning committee met for the second time. The parish resource reports allowed the parishes to present their programs in detail and to share their strengths and limitations with one another. Key words describing the strength or limitation were written on colored paper and taped to the wall. This helped participants form a picture of the advantages that others would bring to the cluster.

The agenda for this meeting includes three tasks: first, to prioritize the strengths and limitations of the proposed cluster; second, to initiate a discussion of the plan for clustering; and third, to appoint a committee to draft a plan for clustering.

The plan for clustering was introduced by the facilitator, who explained that the plan would employ the parameters for clustering outlined in the cluster guidelines. Further, the plan would incorporate the episcopal vicar's expectations for the cluster. The plan would form the basis of the written cluster agreement.

A generic model of a cluster agreement is provided in the cluster pastoral planning guidebook. The model, developed by the Diocese of Green Bay, Wisconsin, includes generic constitutions and bylaws for clusters. Variations of the generic model are also included in the guidelines to show how other clusters resolved staffing questions, Mass schedules, and budget issues. However, each cluster agreement is unique to the cluster that developed it, reflecting the work of the parishioners whose lives will be affected by the agreement.

Given all of this information, members of the cluster pastoral planning committee began to see how the parishes might come together. They talked about the impact of clustering and how they thought parishioners might respond to it. At the end of the meeting they formed a subcommittee to draft a plan for clustering in the two months before the third meeting. The plan would include:

- a general description of the proposed cluster model;
- a description of activities/programs and projects planned for the cluster;
- staff to be hired;
- a demographic picture of the cluster;

- a description/projection of what the cluster might look like in five years; and

- a structure to ensure an ongoing planning and decision-making process for the cluster.

Also, between the second and third meetings of the cluster pastoral planning committee, members reported the results of the second meeting to their parish councils. With their parish councils they reviewed the parish resource reports, including the strengths and limitations of the cluster. They summarized the impact of the cluster on their parish, sketched ideas for starting the cluster, reviewed other cluster agreements, and initiated a discussion about clustering with parishioners.

The Third and Fourth Meetings

Major issues in the third meeting are: staffing, budgeting cluster expenses, sharing religious education and other programs, and developing a Mass schedule for the cluster. In the case of the five-parish cluster, the sub-committee had two assumptions: first, that two priests and a pastoral associate would serve the cluster; second, that one business manager would serve the whole cluster. The duties of the pastoral associate would include assisting the pastor with various pastoral activities and providing guidance for volunteer religious education coordinators.

These assumptions troubled some members of the cluster pastoral planning committee. Their concerns revolved around two issues: the new Mass schedule and the workload of the bookkeeper. They could not see how one person would do the work that currently occupied five part-time bookkeepers. Their concerns led to a decision to take the proposed plan for clustering to the parish pastoral councils for further conversation. This led to a fourth meeting.

The parish pastoral councils discussed the proposed plan. Even though some members still had concerns they agreed to proceed with the plan.

The draft plan for clustering was accepted at the fourth meeting with a few minor amendments. The five parish councils signed the plan and forwarded it to the episcopal vicar. Then it was approved by Archbishop Hanus.

The Fifth Meeting

The final meeting of the cluster pastoral planning committee celebrated the committee's work. The new cluster was named "Penta-Parish" to reflect the first five-parish cluster in the archdiocese. Plans were made to inform parishioners and the general public about the plan for clustering and to extend hospitality to parishioners from other clusters. A search committee was formed to develop a job description and hiring process for new staff. And a meeting schedule was set up for an ongoing cluster council.

The purpose of the cluster council is to assist the pastor by consulting on all that pertains to the mission of the parishes and to streamline the administration of a multi-parish cluster. Councillors provide vision, promote accountability, ensure networking, and believe in the mission. Archdiocesan guidelines define the responsibilities of the cluster council as:

- Providing leadership to oversee development of collaborative services and to share the expenses thereof;

- Formulating policies that establish goals for the cluster that witness to gospel values consistent with the teachings of the Catholic Church;

- Formulating policies to foster good communication;

- Developing and implementing procedures to address policies;

- Serving as a visible sign of the church's efforts to call forth the gifts and talents of its members;

- Engaging in shared responsibility;

- Assessing the common pastoral needs of the clustered parishes, determining pastoral priorities, and developing a long-range plan for the cluster;

- Implementing a cluster mission statement that embraces the life and mission of the cluster parishes so that faith, knowledge, wisdom, ministry, and responsibility are shared for the well-being of the entire community.

The first members of the cluster council were members of the cluster pastoral planning committee who wanted to continue to serve the newly formed cluster. New members will be chosen from the five pastoral councils when their term of office expires. In general, parish pastoral councils meet every month; the cluster council meets every other month. Some cluster agreements suggest specific areas or topics for the cluster council's attention. Most clusters indicate an intention to respect the work of the pastoral councils in their cluster deliberations.

When a pastor is responsible for a multi-parish cluster the archdiocese urges him to use prudent judgment in attending pastoral council meetings. Often staff members attend in the pastor's place, especially in four- or five-parish clusters.

Finance councils remain in place in every parish. Cluster agreements indicate a variety of ways that parishes share the costs of the cluster. Shared costs are discussed at cluster council meetings and cluster costs become items on each parish budget.

Evaluation

The final step in planning is evaluation. Pastors of clustered parishes evaluate progress in regular reports. Six months after the five-parish cluster was established, Father Landherr looked upon it with satisfaction. In his report to the dean he wrote:

> Overall, I believe our process of clustering has continued to go quite well. As you know, we were able to fill both the positions of pastoral associate and cluster bookkeeper with well-qualified and competent persons. This has relieved me, as well as our parish coordinators of religious education, of a fair amount of administrative tasks.

Summary of the Cluster Planning Process

Planning is a response to a concrete situation, not a theoretical exercise about the abstract. The cluster pastoral planning process undertaken by the Archdiocese of Dubuque illustrates this well.

From the beginning, the archdiocese was driven by two factors. One, a negative factor, was the shortage of priests. The other, a strong positive factor, was the call of John Paul II for the whole church to renew itself in preparation for the Jubilee Year. These factors shaped the planning process.

Planning began with large-scale consultation within the archdiocese.

Clergy and laity involved in a variety of ministries came together to study how the archdiocese would respond to the Millennium call for revitalization. From these meetings came speak-out sessions, the articulation of areas of strategic concern, and, finally, *Vision 2000*. Implementation of *Vision 2000* called for a process for clustering parishes.

The first steps in developing a process for parish clustering involved creating the cluster planning task force. This group defined what a cluster is, established parameters, and affirmed criteria for the clustering process. A cluster was defined in terms of collaboration and sharing among parishes. Archdiocesan cluster guidelines expressed parameters, such as the need for professional staff for the cluster. Descriptive statements about healthy parish life were adopted to help parishes discuss their strengths and limitations in the clustering process. With these documents as the foundation for planning, the process was ready to move forward.

Archdiocesan officials identified the five parishes of the cluster now cared for by Father Landherr as a potential cluster and invited members of the parishes to participate in the clustering process. Many factors influenced the success of their effort. One factor was the spirit of collaboration that infused the process. Another factor was the mutual respect, understanding, and trust that emerged among members of the cluster pastoral planning committee. A third factor was the well-designed process that gave everyone a clear role and an opportunity to participate. Communication, a fourth factor, gave everyone in all five parishes access to information, minimizing rumors and allaying fears. A fifth factor was the clear purpose of the process, supported by archdiocesan documents, a realistic timeline, and well-planned meeting agendas. Finally, sufficient resources were committed to the project, including the participation of key archdiocesan officials and skilled staff members.

Conclusion

Dubuque's planning process has been a journey of faith. When it began, none of us knew where it would end. We only knew that we could not remain as we were. The difficulty of setting off on an unknown planning road has been well expressed by Sister Helen Marie Burns, the past president of the Leadership Council of Women Religious. She wrote:

> The past offers no hope of return. The future suggests no promise of
> arrival. Attentiveness to the journey becomes an important activity, but
> always in reference to the unknown rather than the known.

The journey of pastoral planning taught the archdiocese not to distribute clergy to multi-parish assignments without offering supportive
structures and resources. To do so neither respects the human needs of
the clergy nor achieves the strategic goal of "vital communities of faith
in all parishes, including those without a resident priest." Competent staff
to assist the pastor, structures to promote the sharing of programs, and
resources and opportunities to work collaboratively with other parishes
are all important factors in achieving our goal. They foster new and creative pastoral life in the parishes.

Dubuque's planning process, begun in the mid-1990s as a response
to declining numbers of priests and the Holy Father's call for a "new
springtime" in the church, became an exciting, life-giving exercise in
shared responsibility. Far from seeing the future as a series of grim
choices, parishes undergoing this process discover a future of unexpected possibilities. The process called forth leaders to provide vision and
faith in the mission as they develop new structures for parish life.
Parishes, able to recognize goals that relate to their own concerns, have
been enthusiastic in responding to the goals and strategies.

We have been called to new ways of thinking, to creating a new way
of being church. Archbishop Rembert Weakland has written:

> Every generation of history has had to face new problems, the answers to
> which were not among the issues that Jesus talked about with his disci-
> ples. We can readily understand why: as times would change, new inven-
> tions would demand new thinking.

Cluster councils are one response to the call for new ways of thinking. Cluster councils, working with pastoral leadership, facilitate the revitalization of parishes. They help bring to life a new vision for all of the
parishes within the cluster.

Cluster councils themselves serve as a means of networking, not only among the parishes in the cluster but with the wider church and the community. Members of the cluster council function as true leaders: they believe in their mission of inviting others to accompany them in accomplishing their goals. They facilitate a new way of being church. This was well expressed at the end of a cluster planning meeting by a parish council chairperson. "We should stop using the word 'limitations,'" said the chairperson. "There isn't one of us sitting around this table who doesn't realize that clustering will make all of our parishes better off than we are right now."

CHAPTER TEN

The Culturally Integrated Council

Mark F. Fischer and María Elena Uribe

St. Lucy Church in Long Beach, California, has had a "Vietnamese Pastoral Council" for many years. It conducts its discussions in Vietnamese. The council is separate from the parish pastoral council, in which English is spoken. The pastor of St. Lucy's, Father Michael Roebert, cannot participate in the Vietnamese Pastoral Council. He does not speak the language. He asked the elders to send a representative to the English-speaking council, which they did. But Father Roebert still wishes that he could participate in the Vietnamese council.

Father Roebert faces a problem that is increasingly common in U.S. Catholic parishes. He wants to consult his parishioners by means of a pastoral council. He knows that, unless he learns about their pastoral reality, he cannot serve them as well as he wants. But multiple languages make communication difficult. And even in a parish where councillors speak the same language, they often stem from different cultural traditions. These traditions make different assumptions about the way members understand the council and relate to the pastor. His solution is to maintain more than one pastoral council, even though canon law implies that parishes should have only one.

Almost every parish pastoral council in the U.S. is multicultural in at least one sense. Almost every council is composed of people with different cultural roots. If that is what "multicultural" means, then it is almost meaningless to speak of multicultural councils. We might as well speak of all councils.

In this chapter, we will narrow our focus. Here we will speak of the multicultural pastoral council as a council with a large percentage of immigrants. Then we are speaking of a distinctive kind of council. On it, the native language of many councillors (and even of the pastor) may not be English. This is increasingly common. According to a recent study, one in five U.S. parishes celebrates two Sunday Masses in a language other than English each week.[1] Such "immigrant councils," especially when the immigrants are new or recently arrived, present distinctive cultural challenges.

1. One challenge is the monocultural council. That is the council in which the majority of members belong to a single culture different from that of the pastor. Indeed, the pastor may be the immigrant.

2. A second challenge is the bicultural council. In this council, two cultures make up the majority of councillors. One culture may not be made up of immigrants and may dominate the other.

3. A truly multicultural council is a third challenge. In this council, members include immigrants from a variety of countries.

The "multicultural council" is not necessarily the multilingual council. People from different cultures may speak a common language. The description of any pastoral reality can be translated. That is why we define the multicultural council in terms of immigration, not language. For our purposes, the multicultural council is one in which a large percentage of members are immigrants. They may have had no experience with structures of church consultation in their native land. They may not have been in the U.S. long enough to be familiar with church consultation as we practice it. And a pastor may not know the culture of his councillors well enough to enter into dialogue with them.

In this chapter we shall examine the meaning of the multicultural council and shall make an argument for cultural integration. Although such multicultural councils pose communicative challenges, their basic dynamic—the search for wisdom—remains the same. We shall look at the purposes of the culturally integrated council, at the meaning of consultation, and at the selection of members. But we do not advocate separate pastoral councils for each parish immigrant or ethnic group. That will become clear in the next section.

Separate Pastoral Councils?

To be sure, some parishes have established separate pastoral councils for each ethnic group. They claim that separate councils can better meet the needs of parishioners than a single parish pastoral council. But canon law makes no explicit provision for multiple pastoral councils in a single parish. Moreover, it is not clear that establishing separate pastoral councils for different ethnic, linguistic, or cultural groups is permissible or helpful. Indeed, well-meaning cultural sensitivity may backfire.

For example, a woman, born in Mexico but living in Los Angeles, said that her pastor's efforts to be culturally inclusive almost divided the parish. "In the parish where I was married," she said, "the congregation was once evenly balanced. One-third were Anglo, one-third African-American, one-third Hispanic: Then more Hispanics moved in and many Blacks and Anglos moved out. The pastor loved us Hispanics. He began to cater to us. He started to do most of the liturgies in Spanish and established a separate Spanish-speaking pastoral council. That drove many of the remaining African-Americans away and turned off the Anglos. Indeed, it alienated some Hispanics who were more comfortable in English than in Spanish. We had to tell the pastor to stop. If he celebrated in English, we told him, most of us could participate."

Eventually this pastor restructured the "Hispanic pastoral council" as a Spanish-speaking "Comite Pastoral" and created a single multicultural council with European-American, African-American, and Hispanic members. But it took some years for people to get over the tensions caused by the well-meaning pastor.

This story illustrates some of the problems with separate ethnic pastoral councils. From them, the pastor may receive different and conflicting advice. The establishment of multiple councils needlessly complicates the parish search for practical wisdom. It can impede pastoral planning. A culturally integrated council is better, for in it all cultural groups have a voice.

The only Vatican text devoted entirely to pastoral councils states that pastoral council members should be representative, but not in a juridical sense.[2] Council members "represent" in that they offer a witness or sign of the entire people of God. Some diocesan guidelines even call for pastoral councils to reflect the parish population in terms of gender, age, and economic and educational background. More important than mirroring a demographic profile, however, is making present the community's wisdom. The primary duty of councils is to make present the wisdom and common sense of the people of God. We believe that a single council can do this. For two reasons the establishment of separate pastoral councils for the various ethnic groups in a parish is not necessary or desirable.

First of all, no official document makes provision for separate pastoral councils within a single parish. Second, the existence of separate councils may aggravate cultural divisions already existing in the parish. Different groups may give the pastor conflicting advice. When there are many councils, there is no one forum in which to iron out differences. For that reason, we recommend a single parish pastoral council. We believe that a single council can represent the parish and accomplish the planning task, even in multicultural parishes. "If a pastor needs an ethnic advisory board, let him establish one," said one Filipino man. "But don't call it a pastoral council."

The Threefold Purpose

A pastor should undoubtedly consult his people, even when he does not speak their native language. In that case he must seek parishioners who can translate. We will discuss this below in connection with member recruitment. For the present, let us say only that pastors need not speak the native language of every councillor. More important is the ability to draw them into the work of the pastoral council.

Every pastoral council has the same basic purpose. "It is to investigate under the authority of the bishop all those things which pertain to pastoral works, to ponder them and to propose practical conclusions about them."[3] This is the way that Vatican documents generally speak about pastoral councils. They were first envisioned at the diocesan level, and then promoted at the parish level. The threefold task of councils may be described as pastoral planning. It is to study a pastoral issue, reflect on it deeply, and recommend conclusions. Within this threefold task, councillors exercise leadership.

At times, however, we confuse councillors by calling them leaders. In the Spanish language, the word "leadership" ("liderazgo") may have a different connotation than it does in English. For some Mexicans, and Central and South Americans, "el líder" is an individual who takes control, who bears the brunt of responsibility, and who tells people what to do. "In my culture, the term 'leader' can have a negative meaning," one Mexican man told us. "The leader is the one with power, the one who commands others, the one who gets things done." Leadership exercised in the council is different. It means service. U.S Catholics are proud to call themselves leaders, for the English word lacks the negative connotations of the Spanish. When English speakers tell new council members from Mexico that they are "leaders," the immigrants may feel that the term is unrealistic, presumptuous, or incompatible with church service.

In that case, the pastor needs to show what leadership on the council really means. It does not mean that the laity take over and sideline the pastor. It means that everyone contributes to the pastoral-planning task. One layperson may chair the group. Another may establish an ad hoc committee. A third may serve as secretary. Over all these activities, the pastor presides. He is doing the consulting.

Some pastors find it difficult, however, to define what they are consulting about. In years gone by, they would form councils without any clear plan in mind except to increase the participation of parish members. In light of canon law, however, they now have definite expectations of the council. What pastors expect is helpful investigation, thorough pondering, and sound conclusions. In short: pastoral planning.

Yet even those pastors who understand planning occasionally find it hard to communicate with their councillors. Misunderstandings of the parish pastoral council's threefold task are common. Some councillors wrongly believe that the "investigation" done by a pastoral council requires advanced technical training. They think that one must be a professional planner to be on the council. This is not true. Pastors can help them see that the word investigation can also mean visiting, learning, studying, and seeing for oneself.

Others mistakenly expect the pastoral council to be as efficient as a Fortune 500 company. They do not realize that "pondering" (the work of reflection) takes time. A Filipino woman remarked, "In the USA, we have a culture of efficiency—instant soup, instant coffee, even instant babies." She rejected this assumption in the pastoral council. "In the pastoral council we discover that we have to slow down and 'ponder' things." The prudent pastor reaches important decisions slowly, after weighing all the facts.

Still others may be confused about the authority of councils. They may think that a council possesses deliberative vote or legal power. But strictly speaking, councillors are to recommend practical conclusions to the pastor. They do not legislate.

The Meaning of Consultation

Vatican documents state that the council enjoys a consultative vote only. But consultation can mean different things, depending on the culture of the councillors. Consider, for example, the following story about St. Anne church (the name has been changed) in Orange County, California. This church has had a sizable Vietnamese congregation since the fall of Saigon and the exodus of Vietnamese to America.

A Vietnamese-American seminarian, anticipating his ordination this year, recently began to plan his first Mass. He approached St. Anne church, his parents' parish. The pastor, a U.S.-born priest, referred him to the "Vietnamese pastoral council." The council was used to operating with autonomy in the parish's Vietnamese affairs. The council "president" (he was not a "chairman") insisted:

- that because a bishop was to be present at the first Mass, all liturgical plans had to meet the pastoral council's approval;

- that only the parish's own Vietnamese choir could sing; and
- that the council president, as the community elder, would be expected to address the congregation at the conclusion of the newly ordained priest's first Mass.

The restrictions placed by the council offended the seminarian. He consulted his parents. With their approval, he decided to celebrate his first Mass in another parish.

Reflecting on the "pastoral council" of St. Anne Church, we can say this: the distinction between consultation and implementation was by no means clear. The U.S.-born pastor had presumably found the Vietnamese council trustworthy. He had consulted it in the past and had valued its recommendations. Over time, he had invited the council members to organize Vietnamese community events in the parish. This may be legitimate. But it is not the way Catholics usually understand consultation. In a consultation, there is give and take between the pastor who consults and the people whom he consults. The pastor must accept the council's recommendations before they are implemented.

We believe that the distinction between consultation and implementation is fundamental. When a pastor consults the council, he seeks wisdom. The search for wisdom is different from wise action. It comes first. After a decision has been made, it is time to implement it. To be sure, the same group may do both. The pastor may make the decision in concert with the council and then ask the council members to carry it out. But strictly speaking, the search for wisdom (consultation) differs from the resulting action (implementation). When councillors implement a decision, they do so as volunteers under the direction of the pastor—and not as the pastoral council.

The distinction can also prevent embarrassment and bad feelings. Consider the following story. In a large California diocese, the number of Korean Catholics has grown enormously. The community was assigned a U.S.-born priest, who developed a pastoral council. When the pastor was reassigned, the council continued to meet in the priest's absence and make decisions for the Korean Catholic community—something for which canon law makes no provision. Community leaders even invited a bishop from Seoul to visit and confirm their children. When the local diocesan bishop heard about the invitation, he had to explain to the Koreans that the bishop from Seoul did not have permission to administer confirmation in his diocese. It was an embarrassing moment. Councils have a consultative vote. They cannot make decisions on behalf of the parish or ethnic community.

The Meaning of "Pastoral"

Councils investigate, ponder, and propose conclusions about "pastoral" matters. In this way they "foster pastoral activity." But what are these pastoral matters? In Spanish, the word "pastoral" has a distinctive meaning. Spanish speakers talk about "pastoral de litúrgica" and "pastoral de evangelizadora." "Pastoral" is a noun that connotes ministry, catechesis, religious service, spirituality, and coordination of parish events. For that reason, many people think that "pastoral" councils should have nothing to do with the business of parish administration.

For U.S. Catholics, however, "pastoral" is an adjective. It means "pertaining to the pastor"—something different and arguably broader than the Spanish "pastoral." To be sure, pastoral matters include traditionally "spiritual" matters, such as catechesis and liturgy. But it is not limited to spiritual matters. It can also mean temporal affairs, fund-raising, and the technical skills of the trained planner. The documents of the church do not assign spiritual matters to one council (the pastoral council) and administrative matters to another (the finance council). Indeed, the matter of the pastoral council includes anything the pastor sees fit to consult about except matters of faith, orthodoxy, moral principles, or laws of the universal church.

Today, many North Americans speak of the "pastoral" council as a planning body. It plans along the lines of canon 511, that is, by "investigating," "pondering," and "making recommendations" about pastoral matters. Indeed, many pastors are so committed to the planning paradigm that they ask councillors to express their advice in terms of goals and objectives. About this North American "pastoral" council, the Latin American may be puzzled. To him or her, a "consejo de pastoral" is relational and ministerial, not a matter of goals and objectives. Goals and objectives—the search for them may seem formal, technical, and artificial.

Here the possibility of cultural misunderstanding is great. Every pastoral council seeks practical wisdom. But not every council investigates and ponders the same matters. Not every council forms its conclusions in the same way. In order to prevent misunderstandings, pastors should clarify what they seek. If they want the council to express its conclusions in terms of goals and objectives, they should say so. If they want the council not only to plan, but actually to coordinate a parish event, then they should explain. The basic rule of thumb is this: pastors do the consulting. They have to tell their councillors what they seek.

Selection of Members

Not every parishioner, however, is able to understand the pastor's search for wisdom. Not every parishioner can understand the work of investigation, pondering, and drawing conclusions. Pastors who encourage parishioners to join the pastoral council merely because they can "represent" a particular ethnic group may do the parishioner a great disservice.

Indeed, the very notion of a pastoral council may be incomprehensible to the immigrant. Poor immigrants may believe that they are incapable of advising a priest. They may feel that they not only lack the education, but also are unworthy. They are reluctant to offer advice to one who, in their native village, directs them spiritually, politically, and economically. "Many of my poor countrymen are like the laborer I hired to help with construction work," said a Mexican-American woman who was a pastoral council chairwoman. "He hung his head and would not meet my eyes."

The fundamental criterion for potential councillors is this: are they able to accomplish the council's work? In other words, are they able to seek the truth together, reflect on and discuss it, and draw sound conclusions? If they can do this, they may be good council members. But discovering this talent takes time. Potential councillors have to learn about councils. They have to understand what being a councillor entails.

For that reason, we advocate a process of sharing wisdom[4] about member selection. According to this process, the selection of council members requires accurate information and sound discernment. In choosing persons for the pastoral council, parishes should invite all who are interested to a series of meetings. The meetings are designed to educate people about the purpose of the council. They also enable parishioners to discern together who is suited for the work of the council. Parishioners work together as equals, for all share in the wisdom of the community.

Cultural misunderstanding, however, may cripple the shared wisdom process. Good intentions about sharing wisdom do not suffice, especially in a bicultural situation where one culture is more powerful than another. This was the case at St. Julie Church, where Father Sean O'Rourke wanted to establish a council. He taught the parishioners about the principle of shared wisdom. Prominent leaders at St. Julie's, born in the U.S., wholeheartedly affirmed the principle. In order to select councillors, they advertised open meetings. They invited the participation of all by means of announcements in the bulletin. They assumed that they were being fair and inclusive.

But without intending to do so, the U.S.-born leaders at St. Julie (the name has been changed) overpowered the Mexican-born immigrant parishioners. The Mexicans did not rely on the bulletin for information. They were not familiar with the concept of open meetings. They did not know how to participate in them effectively. The very process of the meetings favored the U.S.-born and suppressed the wisdom of the immigrants. When the council members were elected in the last of three open meetings, all but two were born in the U.S. And the two Mexican-born councillors were invariably quieter than their U.S.-born counterparts. Many Mexican parishioners were resentful.

Father O'Rourke wanted to share wisdom successfully in his bicultural situation. He and the council questioned their assumptions about how councillors should be selected and about how to include others in decision making. They realized that they had to fit the process of selecting councillors to their situation. They had to ensure the participation of all, especially the Mexican parishioners. So the next time they had to choose council members, they adapted the shared wisdom process. Father O'Rourke and his team:

- planned parish meetings with Mexican parishioners, helping them to identify parishioners with appropriate gifts for council ministry;

- created opportunities for faith-sharing with all those present;
- invited parishioners by means of a phone tree, in addition to the bulletin;
- made the meetings hospitable, incorporating Mexican foods and styles of prayer;
- created opportunities at the meetings for Mexican parishioners to meet separately and as part of the whole;
- found ways to express to each cultural group the conclusions of the other; and
- established a climate in which almost half of the chosen councillors were of Mexican descent.

In this way, the council at St. Julie overcame the resentment of those Mexican parishioners who felt they had been excluded. It became a truly bicultural council. St. Julie's parishioners did not choose councillors merely for their cultural background. They chose them for their ability to do the council's threefold work. The best way to choose councillors is to invite parishioners into the selection process so that they can share their wisdom.

Conclusion

Heightened awareness of multiculturalism in today's church has important consequences for pastoral councils. Such councils have a well-defined purpose. It is to make present the wisdom and common sense of the community. Every cultural group goes about this work of pastoral planning in its own way.

We looked, for example, at the distinctive dynamic of the monocultural council whose pastor belongs to a different culture. Sometimes the pastor puts such trust in the council that the council enjoys (even inappropriately) great authority, as in the Vietnamese council of St. Anne church. Sometimes problems arise, as in the case of the Korean council that continued to meet after its American pastor was reassigned. These examples underscore the importance of good communication, especially about the nature of church consultation.

We also looked at the bicultural situation at St. Julie Church. There the

U.S.-born parishioners learned how to adapt the shared wisdom process. The result was a single council composed of members of two cultural groups. More importantly, its members were chosen at an open meeting for their ability to do the work of the council, the work of pastoral planning.

A truly multicultural council was reflected in the Mexican woman's story about her Los Angeles parish. There the well-meaning pastor, in an effort to meet the needs of the Spanish-speaking parishioners, established a separate Hispanic "pastoral council." This separate council proved divisive. Although the pastor eventually fused the Hispanic pastoral council members into a new, multicultural council, it was a difficult process. In order to avoid these difficulties, and to be faithful to the spirit of canon law, we do not recommend separate ethnic councils.

We believe that the church has defined parish pastoral councils in a way that can be translated from one culture to another. Every culture understands the concept of the search for wisdom. Our challenge is not to establish separate ethnic councils that "represent" in a manner foreign to the church's understanding of this word. It is rather to establish well-integrated pastoral councils, councils that pastors who seek wise guidance can successfully consult.

Notes

Chapter One:
Working Together to Build an Effective Parish

1. The source of the figure of 10,000 councils was Charles A. Fecher, *Parish Council Committee Guide* (Washington, D.C.: National Council of Catholic Men, 1970), p. 10. Robert G. Howes estimated that three-fourths of U.S. parishes have councils in "Parish Councils: Do We Care?" *America* 135:17 (November 27, 1976), p. 371. This figure was confirmed by David C. Leege, "Parish Life Among the Leaders," Report No. 9 of the *Notre Dame Study of Catholic Parish Life*, edited by David C. Leege and Joseph Gremillion (Notre Dame, IN: University of Notre Dame, 1986), p. 6. The claim that nine in ten parishes report having a parish pastoral council was made by Bryan T. Froehle, Mary L. Gautier, *National Parish Inventory Project Report* (Washington, DC: CARA, October, 1999), p. 22. The same authors' *Catholicism USA: A Portrait of the Catholic Church in the United States*, Center for Applied Research in the Apostolate, Georgetown University (Maryknoll, NY: Orbis Books, 2000), repeated the 90% figure.

2. Sacred Congregation for the Clergy, "Private Letter on 'Pastoral Councils'" (*Omnes Christifideles*, 1/25/73), par. 9, reprinted in James I. O'Connor, editor, *The Canon Law Digest*, Vol. VIII: Officially Published Documents Affecting the Code of Canon Law 1973-1977 (Chicago: Chicago Province of the Society of Jesus, 1978), pp. 280-288. Also published as "Patterns in Local Pastoral Councils," *Origins* 3:12 (Sept. 13, 1973): 186-190.

3. Mark F. Fischer, "What Was Vatican II's Intent Regarding Parish Councils?" *Studia Canonica* 33 (1999): 5-25.

4. Patrick J. Brennan, *Re-Imagining the Parish: Base Communities, Adulthood, and Family Consciousness* (New York: Crossroad, 1990), esp. p. 18.

5. Arthur R. Baranowski, in collaboration with Kathleen M. O'Reilly and Carrie M. Piro, *Creating Small Faith Communities: A Plan for Restructuring the Parish*

and Renewing Catholic Life (Cincinnati: St. Anthony Messenger Press, 1988), esp. pp. 38, 41.

6. Michael Parise, "Forming Your Parish Pastoral Council," *The Priest* 51:7 (July, 1995): 43-47.

7. Mary Benet McKinney, *Sharing Wisdom: A Process for Group Decision Making* (Allen, TX: Tabor Publishing, 1987; Reprint edition: Chicago: Thomas More Press, 1998).

8. These are the categories of "The Parish in Canon Law," Chapter 5 of James A. Coriden, *The Parish in Catholic Tradition: History, Theology and Canon Law* (New York and Mahwah: Paulist Press, 1997).

Chapter Two:
A Spirituality for Councils

1. National Conference of Catholic Bishops, *Sons and Daughters of the Light: Ministry with Young Adults: A National Pastoral Plan* (Washington, DC: United States Catholic Conference, 1996). [Hereafter *Sons and Daughters of the Light*]

2. National Conference of Catholic Bishops, *Called and Gifted for the Third Millennium: Reflections of the U.S. Catholic Bishops on the Thirtieth Anniversary of the Decree on the Apostolate of the Laity and the Fifteenth Anniversary of* Called and Gifted (Washington DC: United States Catholic Conference, 1995).

3. Loughlan Sofield and Donald Kuhn, *The Collaborative Leader: Listening to the Wisdom of God's People* (Notre Dame, IN: Ave Maria Press, 1995).

4. Canadian Conference of Catholic Bishops, Laity Commission, *The Parish Pastoral Council: Guidelines for the Development of Constitutions* (Ottawa: Canadian Catholic Conference, 1984).

5. National Conference of Catholic Bishops, Committee on Women in Society and in the Church, NCCB. *From Words to Deeds: Continuing Reflections on the Role of Women in the Church* (Washington, D.C.: United States Catholic Conference, Inc. Washington, D.C. 1998). [Hereafter *From Words to Deeds*]

6. Parker J. Palmer, *The Active Life: A Spirituality of Work, Creativity, and Caring* (San Francisco: Harper and Row, Publishers, 1990), p.2.

7. National Conference of Catholic Bishops, *From Words to Deeds*.

8. Walter J. Burghardt, S.J. *Seasons That Laugh and Weep* (New York and Mahwah: Paulist Press. 1983).

9. Interdicasterial Commission of Pope John Paul II, *Catechism of the Catholic Church* (Vatican City: Libreria Editrice Vaticana; and St. Paul Books and Media, 1994), no. *The Catechism of the Catholic Church*, #1767.

10. National Conference of Catholic Bishops, *Sons and Daughters of the Light.*

11. James C. Fenhagen, *Invitation to Holiness* (San Francisco: Harper and Row, 1985).

12. Donald McNeill, Douglas Morrison, and Henri Nouwen, *Compassion: A Reflection on the Christian Life* (Garden City, NY: Image Books, 1983), p. 4.

13. Ibid, p. 13.

14. Jim Castelli and Joseph Gremillion, *The Emerging Parish: The Notre Dame Study of Catholic Life Since Vatican II* (San Francisco: Harper and Row, Publishers, 1987).

15. Loughlan Sofield, Rosine Hammett, and Carroll Juliano, *Building Community: Christian, Caring, Vital* (Notre Dame, IN: Ave Maria Press, 1998).

Chapter Three:
Involving the Right People:
Selecting Parish Pastoral Council Members

1. *The Roman Ritual: Shorter Book of Blessings*, Catholic Book Publishing Co. New York, 1990.

Chapter Five:
Appreciative Inquiry:
A Powerful Process for Parish Listening and Planning

1. For more about this process see David L. Cooperrider, Peter F. Sorensen, Jr., Diana Whitney, and Therese F. Yaeger, editors, *Appreciative Inquiry: Rethinking the Organization Toward a Positive Theory of Change* (Champaign, Il.: Stipes Publishing LLC, 2000). The following presentation of the organizational principles of Appreciative Inquiry is derived from the work of Cooperrider et. al.

2. Cooperider et. al., *Appreciative Inquiry*, p. 5.

3. Wayne Simsic, *Praying with Meister Eckhart*. Companions for the Journey Series (Winona, MN: St. Mary's Press, 1998), p. 21.

4. Mullen Lecture address by Fr. Michael Himes, Cleveland, Ohio, 18 April 1999.

5. See Stephen R. Covey, *The Seven Habits of Highly Effective People: Powerful Lessons in Personal Change* (New York: Simon & Schuster, 1989).

6. The "basic change model" is presented in *The Seven Habits of Highly Effective People Leadership Course Manual*, published by the Franklin Covey Company, 1998, version 2.0, p. 10.

7. Kennon L. Callahan, *Twelve Keys to an Effective Church* (San Francisco: HarperSanFrancisco, 1983), p. xx.

8. For a more detailed discussion, see Cooperrider et.al., *Appreciative Inquiry*, pp. 40-43.

9. Parish planners do not have to use all six questions. They can use just a few if they are constrained by time or desire a shorter process. There is an order and logic to them, however, that should be respected. Also, they should never use question 6 ("Images of the Future") alone. The preceding questions set a context for answering this question, drawing out life-giving images of the parish, reshaping the way the people see the parish. Without this reshaping, no matter how positively worded the last question is, the answer comes out as a gripe list. Framing it within the context of the answers to the preceding questions makes the last question effective.

Chapter Six: Demographic Information as an Aid to Parish Planning

1. Pope John Paul II, *Code of Canon Law*, Latin-English Edition, Translation prepared under the auspices of the Canon Law Society of America (Washington, D.C.: Canon Law Society of America, 1998).

2. The 1990 data is obtained using the 1990 Census numbers. The current year estimates are purchased through a third party database distributed by MapInfo called TargetPro based on raw data provided by The Polk Company.

3. MapInfo Corp. can be contacted for current prices at (800) 327-8627. Their address is One Global View, Troy, NY 12180-8399; www.mapinfo.com.

4. Computer Works, Inc. can be contacted for current prices at (813) 988-0434. Their address is 111 South Riverhills Drive, Temple Terrace, FL 33617.

Chapter Seven:
Planning: Idol or Icon of Pastoral Councils?

1. *The New Catholic Encyclopedia*, 1967 Edition, *sub voce* "Icons," Volume 7, pp. 324-326.

2. George B. Wilson S.J., "Some Versions of 'Pastoral,'" *Church Personnel Issues*, National Association of Church Personnel Administrators (February 1987), pp. 4-6.

3. Bishop John Keating, "Consultation in the Parish," *Origins* 14:17 (October 11, 1984): 257, 259-266, at p. 264. The importance of this distinction is also discussed in James H. Provost, "The Working Together of Consultative Bodies— Great Expectations?" *The Jurist* 40 (1980): 257-281 at pp. 265-266.

4. Bishop John Keating, "Consultation in the Parish," *Origins* 14:17 (October 11, 1984): 257, 259-266, at p. 264.

5. Paul Dietterich, "Leadership for Church Transformation: Two Types of Organizational Change," *The Center Letter* 19:2 (February 1989).

6. Ibid, page 2.

7. These conditions are derived from Alvin Toffler's 1971 book, *Future Shock.*

8. Paul Hersey and Kenneth H. Blanchard defined the four styles of situational leadership in *Management of Organizational Behavior: Utilizing Human Resources*, Fifth Edition (Englewood Cliffs, NJ: Prentice Hall, 1988). A summary of situational leadership that applies it to parishes can be found in Charles J. Keating, *The Leadership Book*, Revised edition (New York and Ramsey: Paulist Press, 1982).

9. Gary Kuhne and Joe Donaldson, "Typical Clergy Work," *Review for Religious Research* 37:2 (November, 1995): 147-163.

Chapter Nine:
Sharing More than a Pastor

1. Schoenherr, Richard A. and Lawrence A. Young, *Full Pews and Empty Altars, Demographics of the Priest Shortage in United States Catholic Dioceses* (Madison, WI: The University of Wisconsin Press, 1993).

2. Flannery, Austin O.P. ed.; *Vatican Council II: The Conciliar and Post Conciliar Documents* (Boston MA: St. Paul Editions, Daughters of St. Paul, 1975).

3. Canon 526.1 says that a pastor is to have the parochial care of only one

parish; nonetheless, because of a lack of priests or other circumstances, the care of several neighboring parishes can be entrusted to the same pastor.

4. The *Parish Resource Study* is available from the Archdiocese of Dubuque, Office of Pastoral Planning, P.O. Box 479, Dubuque, IA 52004-0479.

Chapter Ten:
The Culturally Integrated Council

1. Bryan T. Froehle and Mary L. Gautier, *National Parish Inventory Project Report* (Washington, D.C.: Center for Applied Research in the Apostolate [CARA] at Georgetown University, October, 1999), p. 12.

2. Sacred Congregation for the Clergy, "Private Letter on 'Pastoral Councils'" (*Omnes Christifideles*, 1/25/73), par. 7, reprinted in James I. O'Connor, editor, *The Canon Law Digest*, Vol. VIII: Officially Published Documents Affecting the Code of Canon Law 1973-1977 (Chicago: Chicago Province of the Society of Jesus, 1978), pp. 280-288. Also published as "Patterns in Local Pastoral Councils," *Origins* 3:12 (Sept. 13, 1973): 186-190.

3. John Paul II, *Code of Canon Law*, Latin-English Edition, Translation prepared under the auspices of the Canon Law Society of America (Washington, D.C.: Canon Law Society of America, 1983), canon 511. This canon pertains to *diocesan* pastoral councils. Canon 536 describes the purpose of *parish* pastoral councils, but does so in very brief terms. Through the council, states canon 536, "the Christian faithful along with those who share in the pastoral care of the parish in virtue of their office give their help in fostering pastoral activity." We believe that the language of canon 536 (about PPCs) should be understood in terms of canon 511 (about DPCs). Canon 511 echoes the original language about pastoral councils in the Vatican II Decree on Bishops (at par. 27).

4. Mary Benet McKinney, *Sharing Wisdom: A Process for Group Decision Making*, reprint edition (Chicago: Thomas More Press, 1998). For an example of how this process works, see Michael Parise, "Forming Your Parish Pastoral Council," *The Priest* 51:7 (July 1995): 43-47.

About the Authors

George Cobb

Currently the Director of Planning for the Diocese of Charlotte, George has held that position for the past two years. He has practiced in the field of planning for the past 20 years at the regional and local government level. Over that time he has made extensive use of census and locally generated demographic data to create Geographical Information Systems (GIS), which have been incorporated into over a dozen major planning studies on the local and state level. George is charged with overseeing the development of the 20-year Diocesan Strategic Plan and working with 91 parishes and missions in the development of their own local plans. Using Census and private sources, along with pastoral data submitted by the parishes, he has developed a comprehensive GIS system for the diocese to share with the local parishes—at no charge.

George received his masters degree in Public Administration from the University of North Carolina at Charlotte and also holds a Phi Kappa Phi key. He has been a member of the American Planning Association (APA) since 1982. In 1996 he received his Certificate in Pastoral Planning from CPPCD. George and his wife Kim have two children, Catherine, age 7, and Nicholas, age 5, and are active in their parish.

David DeLambo

David DeLambo has worked in pastoral planning and research for the past 14 years with the National Pastoral Life Center, the Catholic Conference of Indiana, and the Catholic Diocese of Cleveland. He has a Ph.D. in Sociology and a masters in Pastoral Planning and Research from Fordham University. He has authored national and regional studies regarding parish life and ministry, and diocesan organization. His most recent publication, co-authored with Msgr. Philip J. Murnion, is "Parishes and Parish Ministers: A Study of Lay Parish Ministry." He currently serves as consultant for pastoral planning, research, and parish pastoral councils for the Diocese of Cleveland.

Mark F. Fischer

Mark is Professor of Theology and Director of Admissions at St. John's Seminary in the Archdiocese of Los Angeles. Before that he served as Director of the Diocesan Pastoral Council office in the Diocese of Oakland. In 1988 he was Chairperson of the Parish and Diocesan Council Network of the Conference for Pastoral Planning and Council Development. From 1990-2000 he was Editor of "Conference Call," the newsletter of the Conference for Pastoral Planning and Council Development. He is the author of *Pastoral Councils in Today's Catholic Parish* (2001) and hosts a "Parish Pastoral Councils" web site at www.west.net/~fischer.

John Flaherty

John Flaherty is currently the Director of the Office for Research and Planning for the Diocese of Pittsburgh, a position he has held since 1989. Prior to joining the Office in 1986 as an associate planner, John taught English and Religion in a Catholic high school. John holds an MA in Systematic Theology from Washington Theological Union where he passed both his comprehensive and department oral exams "with distinction." In addition to his participation in the Conference for Pastoral Planning and Council Development where he served as researcher and editor for the 1995 publication *Diocesan Efforts at Parish Reorganization*, John is active in the National Association of Church Personnel Administrators and the American Society for Training and Development.

Richard Krivanka

Richard Krivanka has served as director of the Pastoral Planning Office for the Diocese of Cleveland since 1979. He provides consultation, facilitation, and project management services to parishes and diocesan

groups related to planning, pastoral councils, organizational development, research, stewardship, and leadership formation. Rick has an M.S.
in Organizational Development and Analysis from Case Western Reserve
University. He also has done strategic planning with a number of community organizations. In 1995, Rick received the Lumen Gentium Award
from the Conference for Pastoral Planning and Council Development. He
and his wife, Barbara, are the parents of one daughter and three sons.

Mary Montgomery
Sister Mary Montgomery is a member of the Sinsinawa Dominicans. She
has a masters degree in Pastoral Studies from Loyola University, Chicago.
She has served as Co-Superintendent of Schools, Archdiocese of
Baltimore, MD; Adjunct professor, Loyola College, Baltimore (Clustering
of Schools); Superintendent of Schools, Madison, WI; and Executive
Director of Sinsinawa Mound, WI. Currently, she is Director of Pastoral
Planning, Archdiocese of Dubuque, IA, where she serves as Consultant
to Parishes/dioceses in Planning Process. She has also served as vice
chair of the Coordinating Committee of the Conference for Pastoral
Planning and Council Development.

Mary Margaret Raley
Mary Margaret is the retired Director of Parish Planning for the Diocese
of Fort Worth. She has a masters in Religious and Pastoral Studies from
the University of Dallas, a Certificate of Lay Ministry from the Oblate
School of Theology in San Antonio, and a Certificate in Pastoral Planning
from the Conference for Pastoral Planning and Council Development.
She has served as vice chair of the Coordinating Committee of the
Conference for Pastoral Planning and Council Development. Currently,
she consults on planning and pastoral council development with several dioceses as well as with individual parishes.

Marian Schwab
Marian has a Ph.D. in educational systems development. She has worked
with a wide variety of people in this country and abroad (in India, Egypt,
and South Africa) on the development of educational programs, espe-

cially in ministry. She has designed and directed ministry education programs for the Archdiocese of Cincinnati and the Diocese of Houma-
Thibodaux. She works for the Diocese of Houma-Thibodaux in
Louisiana where she directs diocesan efforts in pastoral council development, religious education, evangelization, and lay ministry development. She writes a column for *The Bayou Catholic,* and has published
articles in *Today's Parish, The Priest, Theory into Practice,* and
Educational Forum.

Brother Loughlan Sofield, S.T.

Brother Loughlan is a Missionary Servant of the Most Holy Trinity. He
has served as Director of the Missionary Servant Center for Collaborative
Ministry; Director of the Washington Archdiocesan Consultation and
Counseling Center; and Assistant Director of the Center for Religion and
Psychiatry, Washington, D.C. He is on the staff of the Christian Institute
for the Study of Human Sexuality. Brother Loughlan has worked in over
100 dioceses in the United States, as well as in Canada, Australia, India,
Europe, Africa, South America, Central America, Asia and the Caribbean.

Brother Loughlan is Senior Editor of *Human Development* magazine.
In addition to publishing numerous articles on ministry, he is co-author
of many books. His most recent are: *Collaboration: Uniting Our Gifts in
Ministry; Building Community: Christian, Caring, Vital; Design for
Wholeness;* and *The Collaborative Leader: Listening to the Wisdom of
God's People.* All are published by Ave Maria Press.

Brother Loughlan has served on the faculty of or lectured at the
Washington Theological Union, Georgetown University, University of
San Francisco, The Catholic University of Louvain, and Notre Dame
University. During the last few years, much of his time has been spent
conducting programs of clergy education and providing consultation to
dioceses.

He is recipient of the Lumen Gentium Award conferred by the
Conference for Pastoral Planning and Council Development.

María Elena Uribe

For the past three years Mrs. María Elena Uribe has been Coordinator of the Pastoral Councils Office in the Archdiocese of Los Angeles. She is a bookkeeper and a professional Spanish translator/interpreter. For the past 25 years she has been involved in various aspects of school, parish pastoral planning and budget development. As the Coordinator of the Pastoral Councils Office her tasks include educating parish leaders and parish staff, and the formation and development of pastoral and finance councils. Her work includes the development and implementation of parish pastoral plans, and conflict resolution. She recently created The Pastoral Transition program, a new and very important service offered to the parishes in the Archdiocese of Los Angeles. She was Finance Director for Notre Dame Girls Academy High School. She is married, mother of 4 children, and grandmother to 3 boys. In her spare time she writes short stories, does cross stitching, gardening, and remodeling her house.

George Wilson, S.J.

George Wilson has been with Management Design Institute for 27 of its 30 years. After a 10-year career teaching the theology of the church at Woodstock College, he left the academic world and became a church consultant with MDI in 1972. The continued refinement of processes for generating and maintaining member commitment with dioceses, religious congregations, and other service-related organizations has been the dominant focus of his action-research over these years. He has published articles on organizational development in *Human Development, America,* and the bulletin of the National Association of Church Personnel Administrators. His book, *Blessing Prayers,* was published by Treehaus Communications in 2000.

Bibliography

Baranowski, Arthur R., in collaboration with Kathleen M. O'Reilly and Carrie M. Piro. *Creating Small Faith Communities: A Plan for Restructuring the Parish and Renewing Catholic Life.* Cincinnati: St. Anthony Messenger Press, 1988.

Brennan, Patrick J. *Re-Imagining the Parish: Base Communities, Adulthood, and Family Consciousness.* New York: Crossroad, 1990.

Burghardt, Walter J. *Seasons That Laugh and Weep.* New York and Mahwah: Paulist Press. 1983.

Callahan, Kennon L. *Twelve Keys to an Effective Church.* San Francisco: HarperSanFrancisco, 1983.

Canadian Conference of Catholic Bishops, Laity Commission. *The Parish Pastoral Council: Guidelines for the Development of Constitutions.* Ottawa: Canadian Catholic Conference, 1984.

Castelli, Jim; and Joseph Gremillion. *The Emerging Parish: The Notre Dame Study of Catholic Life Since Vatican II.* San Francisco: Harper and Row, Publishers, 1987.

Catholic Church. *Ritual: Book of Blessings.* Approved for use in the dioceses of the U.S.A. by the National Conference for Catholic Bishops and confirmed by the Apostolic See. Collegeville, MN: Liturgical Press, 1990.

Clergy, Sacred Congregation for the. "Private Letter on 'Pastoral Councils'" (*Omnes Christifideles,* 1/25/73). Reprinted in *The Canon Law Digest,* Vol. VIII: Officially Published Documents Affecting the Code of Canon Law 1973-1977. James I. O'Connor, Editor. Chicago: Chicago Province of the Society of Jesus, 1978. Also published as "Patterns in Local Pastoral Councils." *Origins* 3:12 (Sept. 13, 1973): 186-190.

Cooperrider, David L.; Peter F. Sorensen, Jr., Diana Whitney, and Therese F. Yaeger, editors. *Appreciative Inquiry: Rethinking the*

Organization Toward a Positive Theory of Change. Champaign, Il.: Stipes Publishing LLC, 2000.

Coriden, James A. Coriden. *The Parish in Catholic Tradition: History, Theology and Canon Law.* New York and Mahwah: Paulist Press, 1997.

Covey, Stephen R. *The Seven Habits of Highly Effective People: Powerful Lessons in Personal Change.* New York: Simon & Schuster, 1989.

Deegan, Arthur X., II, Editor. *Developing a Vibrant Parish Pastoral Council.* New York and Mahwah: Paulist Press, 1995.

Dietterich, Paul. "Leadership for Church Transformation: Two Types of Organizational Change." *The Center Letter* 19:2 (February 1989).

Dubuque, Archdiocese of. *Parish Resource Study.* Dubuque: Office of Pastoral Planning, 2000.

Dubuque, Archdiocese of. *Vision 2000, A Vision and Plan for the Archdiocese of Dubuque in the Twenty-first Century.* Dubuque: Office of Pastoral Planning, February, 1999.

Fecher, Charles A. *Parish Council Committee Guide.* Washington, D.C.: National Council of Catholic Men, 1970.

Fenhagen, James C. *Invitation to Holiness.* San Francisco: Harper and Row, 1985.

Fischer, Mark F. *I Like Being in Parish Ministry: Pastoral Council.* Mystic, CT: Twenty-Third/Bayard, 2001.

Fischer, Mark F. *Pastoral Councils in Today's Catholic Parish.* Mystic, CT: Twenty-Third/Bayard, 2001.

Fischer, Mark F. "What Was Vatican II's Intent Regarding Parish Councils?" *Studia Canonica* 33 (1999): 5-25.

Flaherty, John P., Editor. *Diocesan Efforts at Parish Reorganization.* A Report Published by the Conference for Pastoral Planning and Council Development. Clearwater, FL: CPPCD, 1995.

Froehle, Bryan T., and Mary L. Gautier, Center for Applied Research in the Apostolate, Georgetown University. *Catholicism USA: A Portrait of the Catholic Church in the United States.* Maryknoll, NY: Orbis Books, 2000.

Froehle, Bryan T., and Mary L. Gautier. *National Parish Inventory Project Report*. Washington, DC: Center for Applied Research in the Apostolate, October, 1999.

Gubish, Mary Ann; and Susan Jenny, with Arlene McGannon. *Revisioning the Parish Pastoral Council: A Workbook*. Illustrated by Mary Kay Neff. New York and Mahwah: Paulist Press, 2001.

Hersey, Paul; and Kenneth H. Blanchard. *Management of Organizational Behavior: Utilizing Human Resources*. Fifth Edition. Englewood Cliffs, NJ: Prentice Hall, 1988.

Howes, Robert G. "Parish Councils: Do We Care?" *America* 135: 17 (November 27, 1976): 371-372.

John Paul II, Interdicasterial Commission. *Catechism of the Catholic Church*. Vatican City: Libreria Editrice Vaticana; and St. Paul Books and Media, 1994.

John Paul II. *Code of Canon Law, Latin-English Edition*. Translation prepared under the auspices of the Canon Law Society of America. Washington, D.C.: Canon Law Society of America, 1983.

Keating, Charles J. *The Leadership Book*. Revised edition. New York and Ramsey: Paulist Press, 1982.

Keating, John. "Consultation in the Parish." *Origins* 14:17 (October 11, 1984): 257, 259-266.

Kuhne, Gary; and Joe Donaldson. "Typical Clergy Work." *Review for Religious Research* 37:2 (November, 1995): 147-163.

Leege, David C. "Parish Life Among the Leaders." Report No. 9 of the *Notre Dame Study of Catholic Parish Life*. Edited by David C. Leege and Joseph Gremillion. Notre Dame, IN: University of Notre Dame, 1986. See Castelli and Gremillion.

Mattessich, Paul W.; and Barbara R. Monsey. *Collaboration: What Makes It Work, A Review of Research Literature on Factors Influencing Successful Collaboration*. New York: Amherst H. Wilder Foundation, 1993.

McKinney, Mary Benet. *Sharing Wisdom: A Process for Group Decision Making* (1987). Reprint edition: Chicago: Thomas More Press, 1998.

McNeill, Donald; Douglas Morrison, and Henri Nouwen. *Compassion: A Reflection on the Christian Life.* Garden City, NY: Image Books, 1983.

National Conference of Catholic Bishops. *Called and Gifted for the Third Millennium: Reflections of the U.S. Catholic Bishops on the Thirtieth Anniversary of the Decree on the Apostolate of the Laity and the Fifteenth Anniversary of* Called and Gifted. Washington DC: United States Catholic Conference, 1995.

National Conference of Catholic Bishops, Committee on Women in Society and in the Church. *From Words to Deeds: Continuing Reflections on the Role of Women in the Church.* Washington, D.C.: United States Catholic Conference, 1998.

National Conference of Catholic Bishops. *Sons and Daughters of the Light: Ministry with Young Adults: A National Pastoral Plan.* Washington, DC: United States Catholic Conference, 1996.

The New Catholic Encyclopedia, 1987 Edition, *sub voce* "Icons," Volume 7, pp. 324-326.

Palmer, Parker J. *The Active Life: A Spirituality of Work, Creativity, and Caring.* San Francisco: Harper and Row, Publishers, 1990.

Parise, Michael. "Forming Your Parish Pastoral Council." *The Priest* 51:7 (July, 1995): 43-47.

Provost, James H. "The Working Together of Consultative Bodies—Great Expectations?" *The Jurist* 40 (1980): 257-281.

Schoenherr, Richard A.; and Lawrence A. Young, with the collaboration of Tsan-Yuang Cheng. *Full Pews and Empty Altars: Demographics of the Priest Shortage in United States Catholic Dioceses.* Madison, WI: University of Wisconsin Press, 1993

Shorter Book of Blessings. See "Catholic Church. *Ritual: Book of Blessings."*

Simsic,Wayne. *Praying with Meister Eckhart.* Companions for the Journey Series. Winona, MN: St. Mary's Press, 1998.

Sofield, Loughlan, and Donald Kuhn. *The Collaborative Leader: Listening to the Wisdom of God's People.* Notre Dame, IN: Ave Maria Press, 1995.

Sofield, Loughlan; Rosine Hammett, and Carroll Juliano. *Building Community: Christian, Caring, Vital.* Notre Dame, IN: Ave Maria Press, 1998.

Vatican II. "Decree on the Pastoral Office of Bishops in the Church" (*Christus Dominus*, October 28, 1965). Translated by Matthew Dillon, O.S.B., Edward O'Leary, O.P., and Austin Flannery, O.P. In *The Documents of Vatican II.* Austin P. Flannery, General Editor. Preface by John Cardinal Wright. New York: Costello Publishing Company, 1975.

Wilson, George B. "Some Versions of 'Pastoral.'" *Church Personnel Issues.* National Association of Church Personnel Administrators (February 1987): 4-6.

Index

Agenda. See Council, agenda

Anticipatory Principle, 93

Appreciative inquiry, 87 ff.; as approach to planning, 88; five principles of, 90ff.; "4-D" planning cycle, 95; personal interviews in, 97

Baranowski, Arthur R., in collaboration with Kathleen M. O'Reilly & Carrie M. Piro, 18

Basic Change Model, 92

Brennan, Patrick J., 18

Burghardt, Walter J., 32

Callahan, Kennon L., 93

Canadian Conference of Catholic Bishops, 25

Catechism of the Catholic Church. See John Paul II.

Catholic Church, *Ritual: Book of Blessings*, 59

Change, 62, 125; conditions for, 126-9; stages of, 64f.

Charlotte, Diocese of, 102, 105, 106, 110

Christifideles laici. See John Paul II.

Clergy, Sacred Congregation for

the (Vatican), 12-13, 185 (fn. 2)

Clustering of Parishes, 164-66; agreements in, 175

Code of Canon Law (1983), 13, 186 (fn. 3), 189, 169 (fn. 3)

Collaborative Ministry, 26, 48

Community, 25-26

Conference for Pastoral Planning and Council Development (CPPCD), 6

Conference of Major Superiors of Men, 30

Constructionist Principle, 91

Cooperrider, David L., Peter Sorensen, Jr., Diana Whitney, & Therese F. Yaeger, 89, 94

Coriden, James A., 22 (fn. 8)

Council Members (councillors), agents of change, 45; election of, 58; ex officio members, 46; gifts, 44-46, 55; nomination, 54; orientation, 56; as planners, 131-132; roles, need for clarifying, 70, 139; selection criteria, 44; selection of, 3, 19-21, 50, 58, 190

Councils, Pastoral, agenda, 2; apostolic councils, 26; consultative theory, 12-13, 123; coordinating theory, 55, 126; pastoral councils, 2; 13; personal dimension of, 31; planning councils, 3, 125; purpose, 2, 47, 140, 185; scope, 12-13, 22; spirituality of (see entries under "Spirituality"); as "upper room" experience, 24

Councils, Finance. See Finance Councils.

Covey, Stephen R., 91, 132

Criteria for selecting councillors. See Council Members, selection of.

Culture, reflected in council, 31, 48-9, 182ff

Deegan, Arthur X., 6

DeLambo, David, 4, 144, 200

Demographic information, 110-113

Dietterich, Paul, 125-6

Discernment, of councillors, 56; prayers of, 38; reflective activity, 154; See also Council Members, selection of.

Dubuque, Archdiocese of, 161, 163-4, 178

Dulles, Avery, 30

Empowerment Cycle, 66ff.

Evaluation, as part of planning, 160, 178

Experience of parishioners, 74

Facilitator, 69, 75, 146-147, 154

Fecher, Charles A., 11

Fenhagen, James C., 35

Finance Councils, relation to pastoral council, 124

Fischer, Mark F., 2, 13 (fn. 3), 201

Flaherty, John P., 5; as editor of *Diocesan Efforts at Parish Reorganization*, 150, 201

Froehle, Bryan T. and Mary Gautier, 11, 183 (fn. 1)

Guidelines for councils, 45-6

Green Bay, Diocese of, 175

Hanus, Jerome (Archbishop of Dubuque), 162, 176

Hersey, Paul and Kenneth H. Blanchard, 130 (fn. 8)

Himes, Michael, 90

Howes, Robert G., 11 (fn. 1)

Icons, 119

Identity and vision, 66, 75, 82, 150; tools for discovering, 76-82, 143

Implementation, as distinct from planning, 158, 188

Inquiry, appreciative. See Appreciative Inquiry.

Involving the right people, 3, pp. 41ff.

Job of pastoral councils, pp. 9ff.
John Paul II, Pope, 178; author of *Christifideles laici*, 1; author of *Catechism of the Catholic Church*, 33

Kenedy Directory. See *Official Catholic Directory.*
Krivanka, Richard, 4, 144, 201
Kuhne, Gary; and Joe Donaldson, 132 (fn. 9)

Landherr, Clayton, 165, 168, 178
Leadership, by the lay council members, 26; situational, 130ff.
Leege, David C.; and Joseph Gremillion, 11, 37
Liturgy, as model of participation, 121

Management Design Institute, 75, 143, 204
Maslow, Abraham, 26
McKinney, Mary Benet, 20 (fn. 7), 190 (fn. 4)
McNeill, Donald; Douglas Morrison, and Henri Nouwen, 35-6
Ministry, collaborative. See collaborative ministry.
Mission, sense of, 26, 73; statement of, 99

Montgomery, Mary, 6, 202
Mother Teresa of Calcutta, 33
Multiculturalism, in councils, 183

National Conference of Catholic Bishops, *Called and Gifted* (1995), 25 (fn. 2); *From Words to Deeds* (1998), 26, 28; *Sons and Daughters* (1996), 25 (fn. 1).
Notre Dame Study. See Leege and Gremillion.
Nouwen, Henri, 34

Official Catholic Directory (Kenedy Directory), 145
O'Rourke, Maria Rodgers, 6-7

Palmer, Parker J., 28
Parise, Michael, 19-21
Parish staff. See Staff, parish.
Parish Resource Study, Archdiocese of Dubuque, 172 ff.
Parishioners, as stakeholders, 152
Pastor, as the one who consults, 188; as leader, 48-9; as motivator, 51; as presider, 123, 139
Pastoral, meaning of, 12, 25, 120, 163, 189
Pastoral Council, guidelines for. See Guidelines for councils.
Pastoral Council, members. See Council Members.

Pastoral Planning, 1, 3, 5, 13, 25, 39, 47, 117 ff.; arguments for, 134-5; in clusters of parishes, 164, 169-70; exercises for, 141ff.; forming a team, 138; as managing change, 62; process for, 140

Pilla, Anthony (Bishop of Cleveland), 38

Planning. See Pastoral planning.

Poetic Principle, 92

Prayer, 28, 69

Provost, James H. (1980), 128 (fn. 3)

Prudence, 16

Purpose of councils. See Councils, purpose of.

Pygmalion Effect, 91

Raley, Mary, 5, 202

Recommending, as task of councils, 157

Reflection, 25, 27-8, 187

RENEW, 16-18

Research, 4, 85ff.; see Appreciative Inquiry, demographic information.

Roebert, Michael, 182

Sacred Congregation for the Clergy. See Clergy, Sacred Congregation for the.

Schoenherr, Richard A. and Lawrence A. Young, 161 (fn. 1)

Schwab, Marian, 3, 150, 202

Schumer, M. Frances, 6

Scope of councils. See Councils, scope of.

Selection of members. See Council Members, selection of.

Simsic, Wayne, 90 (fn. 3)

Simultaneity, Principle of, 93

Sofield, Loughlan, 2, 203

Sofield, Loughlan; Rosine Hammett and Carroll Juliano (1998), 37 (fn. 15)

Sofield, Loughlan; and Donald Kuhn (1995), 25 (fn. 3)

Spirituality, of councils, 23-29; affective, 32; and Appreciative Inquiry, 89f.; compassionate, 34; focused on growth, 38; forgiving, 37; integrates failure, 33; personal, 31; shared, 29

Staff, parish, number of in council, 15

Teresa of Avila, 34

Toffler, Alvin, 126 (fn. 7)

Trends, parish, 150ff.

Trust, 70, 73

Uribe, María Elena, 6, 203-4

US Census, 105, 111

Vatican II, as impetus for planning, 127; *Laity Decree*, 162; *Bishops Decree*, 13

Vocation, as call, 52; of councils, 103

Weakland, Rembert, 180

Wilson, George B., 3, 120, 140, 143-4, 204

Wisdom, 44, 185

Women, attitudes toward, 26, 48

Of Related Interest

Everything about Parish Ministry I Wish I Had Known
Kathy Hendricks
With humor and a hands-on approach the author focuses on helping parish ministers develop better relationships as well as better ways to manage their work and tend to their own spiritual needs. Some topics covered are time management, planning and consulting, running effective meetings, and making collaboration work.
1-58595-199-4, 160 pp, $14.95 (X-39)

The Heart and Soul of Parish Ministry
Regina Coll

Drawing on years of experience, the author offers theological foundations and practical suggestions about what is truly important in parish ministry such as fostering faith, imaging God and Jesus, being human, church, definitions of ministry, and the spirituality of the minister.
1-58595-182-X, 128 pp, $10.95 (X-29)

Pastoral Councils in Today's Catholic Parish
Mark F. Fischer

Based on careful research, long experience, and engaging pastoral examples, the author offers solid, practical answers to a number of important council questions.
1-58595-168-4, 304 pp, $24.95 (J-98)

I Like Being in Parish Ministry
Pastoral Council
Mark F. Fischer

Mark F. Fischer extends a straightforward invitation to pastoral council members and those thinking of being a part of the council to be informed participants. With practical suggestions and clear definitions, he opens the window on the spiritual as well as the action dimensions of this ministry.
1-58595-176-5, 48 pp, $4.95 (X-09)

TWENTY-THIRD PUBLICATIONS

185 WILLOW STREET • PO BOX 180 • MYSTIC, CT 06355
TEL: 1-800-321-0411 • FAX: 1-800-572-0788
E-MAIL: ttpubs@aol.com • www.twentythirdpublications.com